insight text guide

Yvonne Smith

Ransom

David Malouf

First published in 2010, reprinted in 2012, 2014, 2016, 2017, 2018, 2019, 2020 (twice), 2021, 2022.

Insight Publications Pty Ltd
3/350 Charman Road
Cheltenham VIC 3192
Australia
Tel: +61 3 8571 4950
Fax: +61 3 8571 0257
Email: books@insightpublications.com.au

www.insightpublications.com.au

National Library of Australia Cataloguing-in-Publication entry:
National Library of Australia Cataloguing-in-Publication entry:
Smith, Yvonne, 1951-.
David Malouf's Ransom / by Yvonne Smith.
9781921411649 (pbk.)
Insight text guide.
For secondary school age.
Malouf, David, 1934-. Ransom.
A823.3

Other ISBNs:
9781922378545 (digital)
9781922378552 (bundle: print + digital)

Cover design: The Modern Art Production Group

Printed in Australia by Ligare

contents

CHARACTER MAP

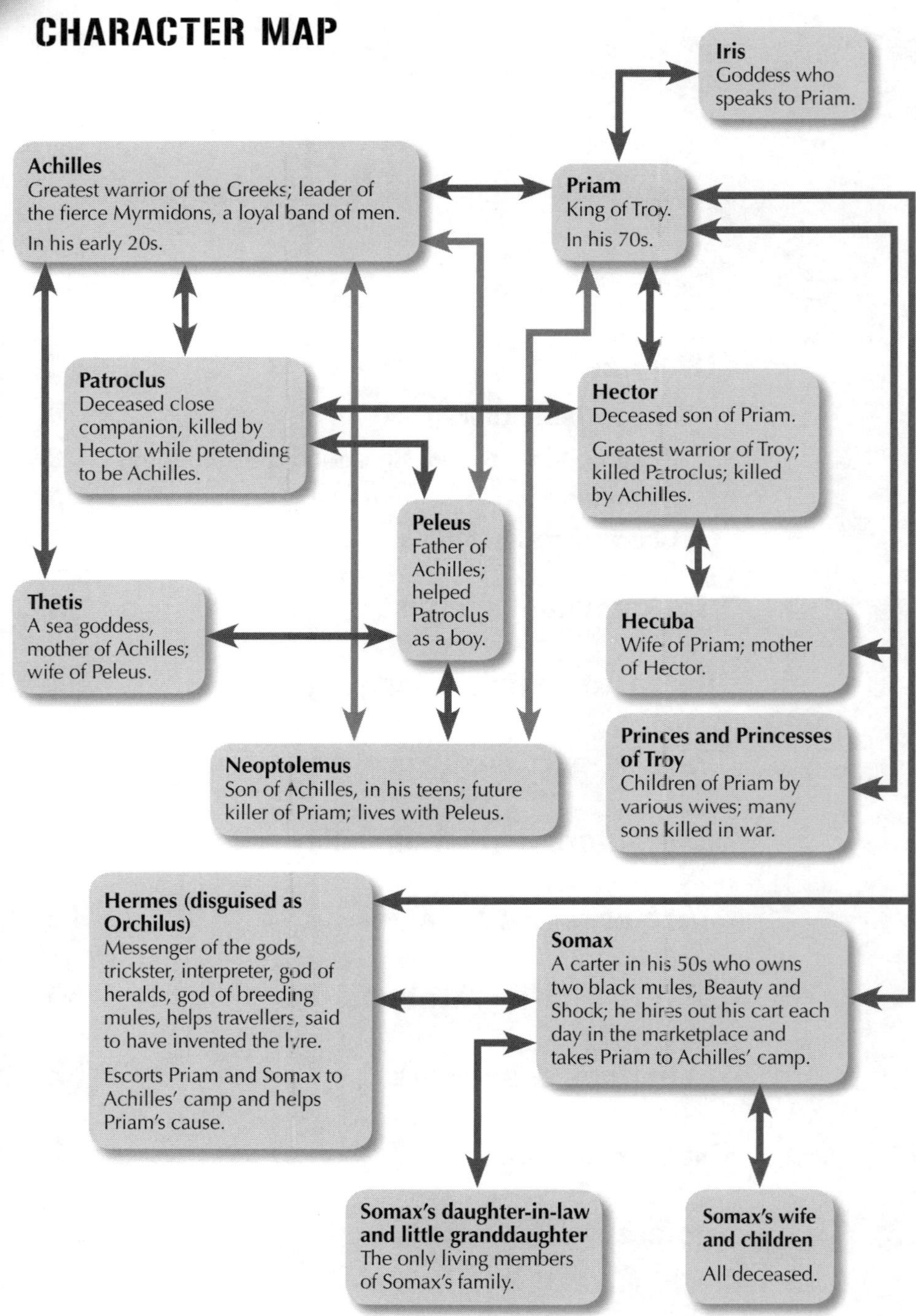

OVERVIEW

About the author

David Malouf is an Australian writer who has achieved significant international acclaim. In addition to winning numerous Australian prizes for poetry and prose, he was awarded the Commonwealth Writers Prize in 1991 (for *The Great World*), the IMPAC Dublin Literary Award in 1996 (for *Remembering Babylon*) and in 2000 his achievement over four decades of writing was recognised with the Neustadt Prize for Literature in the USA. In 2008 he won the first Australia-Asia Award for his *Complete Stories*.

David Malouf was first published as a poet in the 1960s; his first novel (*Johnno*) appeared in 1975, offering a fresh view of growing up in Brisbane. His novels and short stories often explore aspects of Australian identity, society and landscape, blending fiction and history, allowing past and present to speak to each other. He gives his main characters a rich inner life that reveals what really guides their words and actions in the outer world.

David Malouf's career has shown a similar mix of inward focus and outward action. While dedicated to his vocation as a writer, he has been very active in public life in the creative arts in Australia since 1969. He was named an Officer of the Order of Australia (AO) in 1987 for service to literature. He now resides in Sydney and, after five decades of publishing, his career as a fiction writer, poet and engaging public speaker continues to flourish. *Ransom* is his ninth novel and was published in 2009 to wide critical acclaim.

Reading Malouf's work: sound and meaning

It is important to keep in mind that David Malouf is both a poet and a writer of fiction. In novels he pays close attention to structuring an engaging narrative for readers to enjoy, working carefully to express his stories through lively, closely-woven patterns of images (word pictures), rhythms and sounds. In public talks he often reads his poems and stories aloud so the audience can catch the 'music' of the words and phrases. Malouf uses the dynamic, lyrical (song-like, musical) qualities of language to highlight the many shades of meaning in words. To get the most from his writing, read slowly and take the time to feel the flow of the sentences and rhythmic phrases (see, for example, pp.3–4, the opening of *Ransom*). Layers of meaning emerge through images that engage the reader's senses and imagination as the focus subtly shifts from one character's way of experiencing the world to that of another (p.118 is an example). Although it is a short novel, the story of *Ransom* is part of a larger world that the reader can glimpse, as in the brief yet memorable description of Troy (pp.39–40) and the concise evocation of the war-wracked lives of people surviving on the plain outside the city (pp.205–206).

While his novels explore significant ethical issues such as respecting the identity of others, family tensions, war, violence, displacement and loss, Malouf seeks a balanced view of human experience, recognising its mix of light and darkness. His writing often celebrates imagination and creativity in language, together with the quiet joy and uniqueness of each life, human and non-human, including plants and animals. He likes to shape into words experiences that a person may feel deeply but find difficult to express (Priam's unspoken thoughts about why he was 'sorry they had to move on', for example, on p.142). Alongside scenes of hope, Malouf portrays the destructive forces that persist throughout human history and challenge the survival not only of individuals but of cities and civilisations.

Synopsis

The story of *Ransom* is based on the final sections of Homer's famous Greek epic *The Iliad*, one of the earliest poems in western literature. *The Iliad* tells of characters and events during the legendary Trojan War. Malouf once explained that he looked for the 'cracks' and 'crevices' in *The Iliad* where as-yet untold stories might emerge. He found these spaces by creating a more fully realised inner life for his main characters, Achilles and Priam. He also introduces a new character, Somax, who (with his black mules Beauty and Shock) brings to the story a balancing view of everyday life outside of the court or military camp. Beauty's image on the cover of the book is important in this regard. While the meeting between Achilles and Priam remains central, as it is in the final part of *The Iliad*, Malouf presents its heroic qualities in an 'unheroic' manner, highlighting Priam's moral and imaginative courage in choosing to act beyond the bounds of his formal role as king and Achilles' willingness to step aside from revenge and relentless violence to act with compassion.

The action of *Ransom* occurs in the ninth year of the decade-long war between the Greeks (Achaeans) and the people of Troy. The war was caused by the abduction of Helen (wife of Menelaus, King of Sparta) by Paris, Prince of Troy. The novel plays out over one full day and the following morning, although significant events from the years before and after are woven into the narrative. *Ransom* commences on the twelfth day after the death of the Trojan hero Hector, slain by the famed warrior Achilles in revenge for the death of his dearly loved cousin Patroclus. Overcome with grief and anger, Achilles has dragged Hector's dead body behind his chariot each morning for eleven days but the gods keep restoring the corpse so that it looks fresh despite its mistreatment. Achilles feels caught in a web of grief and confusion and wants to break free of it but does not know how. He waits by the sea to hear the voice of his mother, the sea nymph Thetis, who he hopes may guide him.

Meanwhile, Priam, Hector's father and king of Troy, finds that his life is also suspended by grief. He mourns for his son along with Hector's mother, the queen Hecuba, and all the Trojan people. Priam has a vision of sitting in plain clothes on a simple cart pulled by black mules. The cart, he imagines, will take him to Achilles' camp and carry a ransom of precious goods to be exchanged for the body of Hector before returning to Troy for a ceremonial burial.

Despite strong protests from Hecuba and the Trojan court, Priam leaves Troy with the carter Somax and his black mules Beauty and Shock. Somax has been asked to assume the role of Idaeus, the herald and companion of the king. They stop to rest on the way. Hermes, the messenger of Zeus and the god of heralds and interpreters, appears suddenly in disguise and, visible only to the travellers, guides the cart safely past the guards and into Achilles' camp.

Achilles is amazed that Priam has been able to enter the heavily guarded camp. When Priam says he has been guided, Achilles understands that more than human forces are at work. Priam asks for Hector's body so that honourable behaviour can be upheld and Achilles relents, somewhat awed by the old man's presence.

With Hector's body under the cart's canopy, Priam and Somax return to Troy to begin the official mourning period. Achilles has agreed to twelve days of truce before the war resumes. Years later, Somax lives on after the fall of Troy to tell tales about his extraordinary journey but his listeners find it hard to believe him. The mule Beauty seems more important to ordinary folk and they talk of her rather than of warriors and kings. One story is ending and another might be beginning.

Character summaries

The Greeks *(also known as Achaeans; making war on Troy)*

Achilles: The greatest warrior among the Greeks, Achilles is the son of a human father (Peleus) and an immortal sea nymph (Thetis). He fights in King Agamemnon's army against Troy but has little respect for that king. He is the leader of a warrior band called the Myrmidons. Achilles is caught between his desire for a hero's death and wanting a long, peaceful life in his homeland of Phythia in Thessaly. According to prophecy, he is destined to die in the Trojan War.

Statue of Achilles at Sissi's Palace, Corfu, Greece

Thetis: The mother of Achilles and daughter of the sea god Nereus. She is the leader of the sea nymphs (the immortal Neriads) and is married to Peleus.

Patroclus: A cousin and close companion of Achilles, Patroclus was taken in by Achilles' father after accidently killing a playmate. He fights and is killed by Hector while wearing Achilles' armour. His death is greatly mourned by Achilles.

Neoptolemus: The son of Achilles and Deidamia, Neoptolemus lives with his grandfather Peleus after Achilles sails to Troy. Strong, red-haired and trained as a warrior, he is destined to kill Priam, king of Troy.

Agamemnon: King of Mycenae and leader of the Greek army against Troy, Agamemnon is the brother of Menelaus, King of Sparta whose wife Helen was taken to Troy by Paris (son of Priam). A proud, passionate and ruthless leader, he takes the slave girl Briseis from Achilles who then refuses to fight in the Greek army.

Peleus: A respected king, Peleus is the father of Achilles and grandfather of Neoptolemus.

Automedon: A warrior-companion of Achilles, Automedon accompanies Patroclus into his final battle and is with him when he dies. He becomes an aide to Achilles after Patroclus' death.

The Trojans *(defending the ancient city of Troy)*

Priam (a name meaning 'the price paid' or 'the ransomed one'): The king of Troy for many decades, Priam is now in his seventies and aware of his physical weaknesses. He was named Podarces as a child and was saved from slavery by his sister Hesione. He is able to hear and see the gods from time to time and believes they guide him. Priam wants to accomplish a heroic deed before he dies to redeem his self-esteem and be remembered for something other than his savage death.

Hector: The eldest and dearest son of Priam and Hecuba, Hector is a great prince, warrior and hero. He kills Patroclus in battle, thinking he was Achilles, and is killed by Achilles in revenge. Hector is the husband of Andromache and father of the young Astynax.

Hecuba: The queen of Troy and first wife of Priam. Hecuba is the mother of Hector, Paris and many other children by Priam. She is a small, strong, beautiful and determined woman for whom Priam has great love and respect.

Princes and princesses of Troy: Priam has had over fifty children, though many of them have been killed in battle. Those who appear in *Ransom* include the priest Helenus, the prophetess Cassandra, the princes Paris, Hippothous, Dius, Deiphobus, Panyamus and the young Polydorus.

Polydamas: A wise Trojan courtier who advises Priam not to go to Achilles' camp.

Idaeus: The king's herald, Idaeus is Priam's official companion who always travels with him to act on his behalf and speak for him in public. He is replaced by the carter Somax for the journey to Achilles' camp.

Somax: A simple, well-built, rough but rather wise fellow, Somax is a carter. He is about fifty years old. His cart and mules are chosen by the princes of Troy to take Priam on his journey to ransom Hector's body from Achilles. His wife and seven children have all died, but he loves his remaining daughter-in-law (not named) and his granddaughter (also not named). He is very fond of his two mules, especially Beauty.

Animals

Balius and Xanthus: These two immortal war horses were gifts from the gods to Peleus when he married Thetis. They were given to Achilles by his father. Noted for their beautiful appearance, swiftness and high spirits, they pull Achilles' chariot as he drags Hector's corpse in the dust for eleven days.

Beauty and Shock: Two black mules (hybrid offspring of a horse and donkey) who represent everyday life in Troy. They stand in contrast with Achilles' war horses, who belong to the epic world of battle.

The Greek gods *(guiding and intervening in human actions)*

Hermes: The messenger of Zeus (the chief of the gods), Hermes is the god of heralds and interpreters, literature and poets, travellers and borders, and the breeding of horses and mules. He is known to be a trickster and joker. Hermes wears a winged cap and travels at great speed to carry messages from the gods to mortals. He also escorts the dead to the afterlife.

Thetis: A goddess and leader of the Nereids (immortal sea nymphs), Thetis is the mother of Achilles and represents his softer, fluid, more intuitive nature. Her influence has decreased as Achilles has matured and become hardened by fighting.

Iris: Goddess of the rainbow and, like Hermes, a messenger of the gods, Iris appears to Priam in a waking dream (as 'iridescence', p.41) and suggests he think about acting on chance, an idea unheard of in Homer's epic world.

Places

Troy: Also known as Ilium, Troy was an ancient city famous in legend. It was possibly situated in north-west Asia Minor (now Turkey). It is described as a city rising from the plains, protected by a strong, thick wall and gates, with a citadel high at its centre.

The river Scamander: A fertile, fast-flowing river that divides into streams at its estuary on the plain of Troy. It is named after the river-god Scamander who battles Achilles in *The Iliad*. This river is an important place of transition for Priam and Somax and is also the threshold where the god Hermes appears to guide them.

The Greek camp: Situated on the shore of the Aegean Sea, not far from the plain of Troy. Achilles' camp is somewhat separate as he has his own mess hut, tents and guards. The burial mound of Patroclus lies nearby.

BACKGROUND & CONTEXT

Historical setting

Ransom is set during the Trojan War. Scholars are unsure whether the Trojan War was an actual event or a legend that arose from imagined stories told over many centuries, such as *The Iliad*. Excavations at a site in modern Turkey (commenced in 1870 by Heinrich Schliemann and still continuing) have revealed an area where a city like Troy existed over three thousand years ago. The city was destroyed and rebuilt several times. The Trojan War is estimated to have occurred around 1100 BCE.

The Greek poet Homer is traditionally credited with composing two great epic poems, *The Iliad* and *The Odyssey*, which tell the story of part of the Trojan War, its heroes and its aftermath. It is likely that Homer was part of the oral tradition, in which heroic poems were performed by the bard (poet) at social gatherings over several nights. The poems were probably written down around 750 BCE. Homer's poems bring to life the deeds of characters such as Achilles, Hector, Priam, Patroclus and Ulysses. The poems have been passed on, retold and translated for well over two thousand years and are highly valued as foundations of narrative in western literature. In classical Greece they were used as the basis for education, as the stories were thought to explore aspects of moral and practical behaviour.

Homer's poems extended the oral traditions of earlier poets. Before writing became common, stories were told aloud and the storyteller remembered by heart the details of events and heroes' lives. An epic story would often commence when the action was already well underway. Weaving together what had happened before and what would come after were part of the storyteller's art. The greatest desire of kings and warriors was to have their deeds live on in song and story through the coming ages. Stories represented the shared memories of a culture and a storyteller could achieve lasting fame, as occurred in Homer's case, or be regarded as a spinner of improbable yarns, as Somax finds (p.218).

Homer's epic poems feature the actions of the gods and goddesses of Greek mythology. In ancient times they were believed to have significant influence over the physical world and over human affairs. A child, such as Achilles, could have an immortal goddess for a mother and a mortal human for a father. The gods might decide to support a warrior or turn against him. Their unpredictable actions could be motivated by anger and jealousy as well as love and sympathy. They might sometimes choose to appear in human form to communicate with a mortal, then suddenly disappear. The Greeks believed they should be cautious and respectful when dealing with the gods. Their religious ceremonies, sacrifices and offerings were important rituals to honour the gods and seek their favour. Priests and priestesses acted between gods and people and could use visions, dreams, trances and prophecies to seek to know the will of the gods and the future.

Ransom includes important references to divine intervention in the action of the novel. Achilles seeks the voice of his mother the sea-nymph Thetis (p.3) and his horses Balius and Xanthus are a gift from the gods (p.30). The goddess Iris speaks to Priam (p.45–46) and he makes a wine offering to the gods before he leaves Troy (p.101). Hermes appears during Priam's journey (pp.143–158) and ensures the cart reaches Achilles' camp by spellbinding the guards (p.163). The river Scamander (home of a river-god) provides refreshment rather than obstruction (pp.111–115). The music of the lyre with its god-like influence opens Achilles' mind to receive Priam in a favourable way (pp.171–174).

The gods are an important part of the way characters experience the world around them. Achilles and Priam see and hear the gods in their dreams and visions. Whether they are actually real is left open in the novel, especially when Hermes appears to Priam and Somax. He is visible to them and to the mules, yet is invisible to others. His playful behaviour and the way he magically lifts the heavy pole at the entrance to Achilles' camp (p.163) stretch the credibility of the reader yet seem to be part of what is possible in the world of the novel. Rather than a traditional epic, *Ransom* has the feel, at times, of a tale from Ovid, a medieval romance or fairytale. Hermes' appearance draws attention to *Ransom*'s flexible narrative form with its blend of reality and fantasy.

In classical tales, supernatural or gifted companions and mentors may appear to guide the hero as he struggles to reach a place of reckoning with his enemy and to help his return with the 'treasure'. In this case, Priam's quest is to claim the 'treasure' of Hector's body and also the 'treasure' of a redefined identity for himself and Achilles. The physical ransom will be given in exchange for 'treasures' that are beyond material price. Hermes can be seen as part of this tradition, as well as showing the lighter aspects of the gods.

Author's historical context

David Malouf tells how he came to write *Ransom* in his 'Afterword: A Note on Sources' (pp.221–224). He has also given a number of talks and interviews about the novel which are available on websites and as podcasts (see *References*).

Malouf recalls that his first encounter with the Troy story occurred when he was in primary school in Brisbane (p.221). It was 1943 and the world had been at war for four years (he was nine at the time). In his mind he connected the fall of Troy and the way Hector's body was treated with what he and his family saw in newsreels and heard on the radio about the violence in Europe and Asia. After the Japanese attacked the American naval base at Pearl Harbour in 1941, the war in Asia crept closer and closer to Australia. An invasion by Japanese forces was feared. Thousands of allied American troops were stationed in Brisbane as part of the defence of the Pacific region. How would the war end? There was no certainty of an allied victory. Even children could be imprisoned and killed, as the news showed. For the young Malouf it was a fearful time. The Troy story showed him that such difficulties had occurred before and that stories could reflect real life. He understood that a storyteller's imagination could have a powerful and enduring impact on listeners and readers.

As an adult, Malouf has thought a great deal about his childhood and the nature of war. He was politically active in the movement against Australia's involvement in Vietnam in the late 1960s. In the 1972 poem 'Episode from an Early War' he interwove images from *The Iliad* with experiences from his childhood (p.222). He made use of similar thoughts in his novel *Johnno* (p.25), which featured a child who imagined World War II was happening under his bed each night. A seemingly safe world could easily be swept away. He wrote further about the experience of war and its wide-ranging impact on people's lives in his novels *Fly Away Peter* (focusing on World War I) and *The Great World* (about World War II). The short story 'War Baby' (from *Every Move You Make*, pp.91–133) concerns a young conscript, Charlie Dowd, and his experiences at the time of the Vietnam War in the late 1960s. Like Priam in *Ransom*, Charlie feels that he has 'given himself over to hazard, to chance' (p.97) and that he will be deeply tested by his choices.

The influence of war on Malouf's thinking and experience can be felt in *Ransom*, especially in Priam's account of his near-capture and miraculous escape as a child (then named Podarces) when his city was invaded by the fearsome Heracles and his warriors (pp.62–75). It is notable that this section of the novel is Malouf's own elaboration of a much shorter account in *The Iliad* and another early source called *The Library*. By imagining Priam's complex childhood, Malouf creates a more elaborate episode within a 'crevice' of *The Iliad*.

Although *Ransom* was Malouf's first novel in ten years, it was drafted at a time when he was writing poetry and short stories that dealt with complementary themes. The novel has clear connections with several of his earlier works, such as the 1999 collection of *Untold Tales*, including 'Ulysses or, The Scent of the Fox' (pp.47–58). This short story offers another version of the conflict between Achilles and Patroclus and then Patroclus' death, and can be seen as a precursor to *Ransom*. Here, Ulysses plays a more active part – and a cunning, ruthless one – in persuading Patroclus to fight in Achilles' armour so that his probable death will bring Achilles back into the war with Troy. Achilles is shown to be deeply affected by his cousin's death at the hand of Hector because it makes a simulacrum – a living model that is not the actual thing – of Achilles' own desire for a hero's death. Achilles is disturbed that such an act can be made a pretence or mockery. The reverence he has given to heroic death, he realises, may not be worth his life after all. Perhaps he should return home to a long life of peace. It is useful to compare this story with Malouf's different narrative line in *Ransom* where he gives Achilles' anger and impatience a greater role in causing Patroclus to fight in his place (pp.17–19). Achilles' personal conflicts are emphasised in the novel, giving him a greater sense of responsibility for his cousin's slaughter. His grief for Patroclus and anger at himself, objectified in his mistreatment of Hector's corpse, is emphasised in *Ransom* so that Priam's unexpected plea for his son's body provides the chance for Achilles to face his own dark web of emotions and to free himself by acting in a more honourable way.

In *Ransom* both Priam and Achilles must face and overcome dilemmas. Each questions the role he has been playing. The narrative allows the characters to liberate themselves from a crisis of personal values and a loss of self-esteem, something quite different from the view of human action in *The Iliad*.

GENRE, STRUCTURE & LANGUAGE

Genre

Ransom is a work of narrative fiction – a novel – that appropriates (makes use of for its own purpose) the final section of Homer's *The Iliad*, an epic poem. The novel is a form that gives writers great flexibility in taking stories and characters in any direction they choose. *Ransom* takes some of its generic features from the epic and re-makes them in the less formal, freer style of the novel.

Epic

A classical epic is a narrative of great scope, usually with serious themes (such as the founding of a nation or a hero's struggle). The action is set in the past and may involve super-human forces. The epic traditionally uses a formal style of language and may commence in the middle of the action after the narrator asks for the help of a divine muse (one who inspires the speaker). Epics often express the triumphs and failures of human life, relating events with dramatic power as heroes try to overcome the obstacles they face. There is a quality of myth or legend in an epic that raises the narrative and its characters above everyday concerns and appeals to wider human values such as courage, endurance, honour and loyalty.

In *Ransom* the reader encounters epic elements in the historical setting, the focus on Achilles and Priam as heroic (if troubled) characters, the action of the gods Iris, Thetis and Hermes, and the valuing of courage and family loyalty. The novel opens with the action well underway and with Achilles seeking the guidance of Thetis' voice – both recalling the features of epic. The formal language and tone of the epic world is featured in Part II when Priam addresses his court (pp.84–85). Such formality is contrasted with the plain style of Somax (pp.98–99). The restrained forms of address and behaviour between Priam and Achilles when they meet (Part IV) also suggest the etiquette of the classical epic world.

Novel

The novel is a form of literature that developed in Europe in the eighteenth century and took in aspects of earlier narrative forms, such as the epic and tales of romance and adventure. Novels are usually more concerned with everyday life than with legends and heroes, although these may be important in a novel too. As more people learned to read and books became cheaper to produce, the novel became the dominant form in which fiction was published. A novel may be long or short, set in the past, present or future and involve characters from all areas of society. The 'realistic' novel features characters and details created to seem as if they come from 'ordinary life'. A novel may value the anti-heroic, playing down the importance of characters from the higher orders of social and political power. More than the epic, the novel can interweave multiple themes.

Ransom: novel as possibility

David Malouf comments that *Ransom* shows the value of the novel as a literary form because it allows the introduction of what may seem 'irrelevant' to the main action (Writers Series, UNSW, April 2010). He wondered what might happen, for example, when Priam and his new character, Somax, were brought together on a very different journey to the one in *The Iliad*. The novel as a genre allowed him the freedom to explore that possibility which might be left out of an epic. Such details as Priam and Somax talking together by the river Scamander (pp.116–19) enrich the world of the story and also readers' understanding of how and why Priam changes his views in just twenty-four hours. Malouf enjoys the scope and imaginative range the novel allows the writer, while also valuing the great epic works, such as those of Homer, which have been enjoyed and imitated for thousands of years. *Ransom* thus represents a re-working of a long tradition of storytelling. As Malouf comments in the afterword: 'Its primary interest is in storytelling itself – why stories are told and why we need to hear them, how stories get changed in the telling' (p.223). Such a comment encourages the reader to consider the social and cultural forces that are behind stories. As people's likes and beliefs shift over time, literary genres change and the way characters and events are imagined alters considerably.

Structure

The novel is divided into five parts, suggesting that elements from drama shape its structure. The five parts build from the introduction of the conflict (told through Achilles' thoughts) in part I, leading into the complication in Part II of Priam deciding to ransom Hector's body. Priam's journey with Somax and Hermes to Achilles' camp furthers the action of Priam's quest and adds a contrasting pastoral interlude in Part III. The meeting of Achilles and Priam in Part IV is a dramatic climax. A short conclusion in Part V describes Priam's journey back to Troy as the truce begins. The closing focus on Somax as an aged storyteller with his tales about the marvellous journey and his mule Beauty offers a miniature epilogue to the action that recapitulates its lighter interlude in Part III. The closing words of the novel allow the action to connect back to the lives of the listeners and readers. The overall structure of the novel observes Aristotle's preferred dramatic unities of time and place: its main action covers a limited period of one day and night on the plain of Troy.

Tragedy and comedy

While the novel is predominantly tragic, a lighter, partly comic episode is introduced in Part III when Priam and Somax travel together, encountering the god Hermes in disguise. Tragedy is evident in the human loss and failure in a world where characters inevitably face harsh consequences for their actions. Malouf wrote that comedy (the kind that offers a happier view of life rather than being merely funny) 'somehow ... opens the trap and sets us free again' so that 'we get what of course we never get in real life, a second chance' (from his 1973 lecture 'Relative Freedom: *The Tempest*' pp.4–5). By structuring *Ransom* to feature Priam acting by choice – taking a chance to create a fresh possibility – the author introduces a restoring 'comic' element into an otherwise tragic situation.

Language

Malouf's style of writing invites close analysis of the characters' thoughts and actions, together with the features of the world in which they find themselves. There are precise, realistic details (for example, Somax's pikelets made with 'best buckwheat flour, good thick buttermilk', p.118) and evocative moods (as when Achilles feels 'the notes of the lyre continue to colour the air [giving] a dreamlike quality', p.177). Malouf's vocabulary is economical and favours simple terms, although at times he chooses a more complex word that will carry connotations (implied, additional meanings) that enrich the narrative. Water, for example, is not only an element that moves in waves, but is also described as 'shifting' and 'insubstantial' (p.4).

When Priam bathes his feet in the river the reader can share his feeling of being 'nudged and tickled' by the tiny fish who appear like 'little slivers of light ... flashing in' (p.117). Priam is discovering a fresh way of appreciating the small experiences he can enjoy, moments that have been absent from the formalised life of a king. The vocabulary is simple, yet suggests playful ease and excitement, such as a child might sense. In this way the reader is able to experience a theme of the novel: change can come about through small, positive actions, even in times of war.

Shifts in point of view

Subtle shifts in the narrative point of view occur often in *Ransom*. This is a concise way of giving characters an individual presence in the reader's mind. Within a few sentences, the voice of the third-person narrator explains what is happening, then connects with a character's feelings at that moment. At other times, the point of view shifts back and forth between characters. They may be very different in their personalities, social standing and beliefs, but by changing the narrative focus Malouf gives value to diverse (and sometimes opposite) views. In this aspect, his style expresses the theme of tolerance and openness to the unexpected, an important connecting idea in *Ransom*.

Patterns of imagery

Voices

Ransom opens with a personified image of the sea, combining vision and sound: 'The sea has many voices' (p.3). By the end of the novel the reader has encountered a variety of voices through characters such as Priam and Somax. Their internal monologues remind us of the many kinds of 'voices' being woven together to create the story-world of *Ransom*.

Character

It is important to notice the language used to represent Achilles and Priam as being capable in different ways. Achilles has physical prowess, a warrior's skill and relative youth, while Priam is frail with old age yet retains dignity and wisdom.

Achilles is described in terms of his physical qualities such as the strength of his hands and arms ('this corded forearm', p.4). The way he walks, sits and moves is often noted, such as his physical expression of grief at Patroclus' death: 'Sitting cross-legged on the ground, rocking back and forth in his anguish, pouring fistfuls of dust over his head' (p.20). His active mind and deep feelings are made evident to the reader as actions in key moments, such as when he kneels before Priam: 'With a cry he falls on one knee, and leans out to clasp [Priam's] robe' (p.174). His hard nature as a warrior is balanced by language that represents his softer side, influenced by his mother, Thetis. Words such as 'melting of will', 'fluidity', 'shimmering influence', 'the world swims' and 'particles tumble and swarm' (p.172) all suggest an opposite state to his tough existence in the 'rough world of men' (p.6).

Priam is described in restrained, abstract terms that show his self-disciplined nature as a formal, public figure with an exalted role connected to the gods. He 'comes to attention' and 'knows from long experience what is expected of him' (p.41). Priam's old age is expressed in the description of his feet as 'bony and white' and he sometimes winces and feels pain in his joints (p.195) when he moves. Achilles admires his elegant manner and 'the remains in him of a commanding strength' (p.196).

The Elements

Images of water, air, earth and fire are also important in the novel because they show the vital connection between humans and the natural world, helping define how characters think and feel. In ancient times, these were called 'Elements' and were regarded as the basis of all that exists.

Water is associated with Achilles' softer nature and his mother, an immortal sea-nymph.

Earth images point to the productive work of farmers, the harsh conflicts of fighters and the struggle for survival in the daily life of the poor as the Trojan war continues (pp.4–5, p.206).

Air is notable as a cleansing, refreshing influence and accompanies a significant change in a character's thinking (p.188); Achilles 'breathes in its freshness' at the moment he realises that 'the need, the obligation' to torment Hector's body has passed and that 'something in him has freed itself and fallen away' (p.189). Air is associated with the presence of the gods. For Priam, the air 'shimmers with a teasing iridescence' (p.41) just before he sees the goddess Iris.

Fire in the novel is related to war, funeral rituals, death and the future destruction of Troy, as well as the warming heat of the sun (p.206), cooking (p.119) and roasting (p.197) that produces food to eat and share. Priam eats with Somax and later with Achilles, a sign of reaching out to the other person's humanity.

PART-BY-PART ANALYSIS

Part I (pp.3–36)

Summary: *Towards the end of the Trojan War, Achilles faces a crisis that makes him question his whole purpose and identity as a famous warrior.*

Part I opens in the first light of a cold dawn with Achilles hunched up on the shore near the Greek camp, caught in the dilemma of his deep grief and anger after Patroclus' killing by Hector. The fact that eleven days and nights have passed yet Hector's body remains unburied and is being mistreated by Achilles is a catalyst for the plot's development. Although it is written in the third person, the narrative moves into the mind of Achilles, immediately bringing him close to the reader by likening the sea to his mother's womb. The mythical figure of Thetis comes alive as a real presence in Malouf's story-world. We share Achilles' memory of a time that usually belongs to the human subconscious (p.3). Already the powers of remembering and dreaming are felt, both crucial forces in the plot. The reader enters a world of possible enchantments that exists together with what is 'real'. Achilles wants to feel his mother's influence which he hopes will soften his hard nature and help him overcome his dilemma (p.5). His tough, cruel character is challenged at the start of the story by introducing his memories of his childhood and mother.

The narrator uses the technique of flashback to fill in the background of the Trojan War. Achilles recalls many events that have brought him to this point: the past nine years of the war with Troy; his son Neoptolemus; the way Patroclus came to be his close companion before being killed by Hector while wearing Achilles' armour; the appearance of Patroclus' ghost and Patroclus' burial; Achilles' slaying of Hector and dragging the body behind his chariot so all of Troy could see it.

Direct action resumes as Achilles walks back to the camp and notices the men going about their duties, recalling his affection for those who follow him loyally (p.28). They now think he is mad because he still drags Hector's body through the dust each day. The gods restore Hector's body each night so that it looks perfect again every morning (p.31). Again Achilles performs what has become his ritual of rage against Hector. Covered with dust as his chariot returns to the yard, Achilles looks like a dead man himself (p.34). It is as if he is trying to come to terms with his own death in the near future, as well as what has happened in the past. He returns to his hut and goes to sleep, feeling full of 'earth-heaviness' (p.35) in his heart and body. He waits for something to break the spell, to lighten his spirit. He dislikes the rage and despair that is overwhelming him and longs for a new challenge to force him out of his dilemma. By moving the reader through different ways of experiencing Achilles' character and the world he inhabits in Part I (a blend of the real, mythical, recalled and dreamed) we are better prepared to appreciate the strangely intricate, formalised world of the Trojan court that is presented in Part II.

Key point

The reader enters Achilles' mind, rather than just being given a description of his physical strength which was famous in legends. His masculinity is complex and open to 'softening' influences. Achilles is 'filled with his thoughts; his mind, even in its passive state, the most active part of him' (p.8).

Q What is the reader's impression of Achilles by the end of Part I? Are his men correct to think he has gone mad (p.29)? Discuss the evidence and how the reader might decide.

Q Shifts in time are an important part of the narrative structure in Part I. What effect does this have on the way the reader experiences the story? Explain whether you find this an effective introduction to the novel.

Part II (pp.39–107)

Summary: *Priam has been mourning Hector's death for eleven days and nights.*

Daily life in Troy is continuing, despite the war. However, the city now faces a crisis. Its chief warrior-protector, Hector, is dead and Priam the king is aged and weak. Like Achilles, Priam finds his life suspended by deep grief and waits to hear a voice from the gods to guide him out of his quandary. Parts I and II balance each other in this regard, as both Achilles and Priam focus on the violent deaths of people they loved. The answer Priam receives is a surprise (as Achilles, too, will be surprised in Part IV), leading him towards a new way of thinking that is very different to his formal view of life. He will take a chance (p.46). He decides to ransom Hector's body and make the journey dressed simply as a man, rather than a king.

Throughout Part II the reader is alerted to the conscious, deliberate style of Priam in his powerful role. He always acts as he believes a king should. His authority comes from being predictable, not innovative. He values ceremony and self-control in everything he does. At first, we experience Priam as a rather wooden figure but his hidden feelings and memories are emerging. As a father, his extreme grief at Hector's death draws out his strong emotions (p.45), causing him to doubt all he has achieved. He sees himself as 'an ancient doll' reduced again to being prince Podarces, a 'grimed and stinking', abandoned child in an earlier war (p.45). He was saved by his sister, Hesione, from a life of slavery. He became 'Priam', the 'ransomed one', and a king, but his life could have been a different story. This idea of a poor, powerless, alternative existence has troubled him greatly.

Part II gives considerable narrative time to Priam's flashbacks and reflection (pp.63–75) enabling the reader to appreciate Priam's 'inward view' of himself (p.78), as well as his 'outward' persona (how he appears to others). The close relationship between Priam and Hecuba is crucial here, as it is with her that Priam shares his secret fears. They are a loving couple (even though Priam has had many other wives) who both value the positions they have in Trojan society. Hecuba opposes his sudden decision to follow 'chance' (p.61) as she wants him to always behave appropriately. To abandon the appearance of a king is, to her, a kind of madness, echoing the view of Achilles' men in Part I that their leader has gone mad. Crises of leadership play out in the first two parts of *Ransom*, as much as crises of grief.

When Somax and his mules are chosen to take Priam to Achilles' camp, a lighter tone is introduced and the narrative shifts focus from the past into the present (p.102). The suspended action that has stalled everyone breaks metaphorically into the hard-working efforts of the mules pulling the cart laden with treasure at the end of Part II (p.106). The language used to describe the start of Priam's journey suggests that a noble quest is beginning, balancing the tragic tone of Part I and II: 'Whatever it was is over. Or, mysteriously, has just begun' (p.107).

Key point

The description of Troy (pp.39–40) in the opening paragraph repays close reading. The rhythm of the sentences brings together broadly-sketched views and the smallest details. The far view tells us that Troy is a city of 'four-square towers topped by untidy storks' nests, each as tall as a man' (p.39) and the close-up view describes gardens where on a clump of herbs 'snails the size of a baby's fingernail are reborn in their dozens after a storm and hang like raindrops from every stalk' (p.40). The use of alliteration ('t' sounds in the first phrase; 's' 'b' and 'd' sounds in the second) and closely-related vowel sounds ('stork' / 'tall' / 'stalk'; 'snail' / 'nail' / 'rain') connect each detail so that the description is varied yet musical. The reader may sense the connectedness of Troy and its people over a long period of time. Their coming destruction is sadder. A way of life will be lost.

Q Why does Priam decide to undertake such a risky journey? What does this decision reveal about Priam's values?

Q Hecuba fears her husband will be slaughtered by Achilles, as Hector was. She describes Achilles as 'a jackal, that noble bully' (p.57). How does Hecuba's description compare with the way Achilles is represented in Part I?

Q How do the princes of Troy and the courtyard appear to Somax (p.93)? Why is his view of things important in Part II?

Part III (pp.111–163)

Summary: *The day is now drawing to a close on the plain of Troy. The cart travels on and Somax suggests to Priam that they rest and bathe their feet* *in the river (p.111). A charming, swaggering, 'dandified' youth appears and announces he has been sent to escort them to Achilles' camp (p.145).*

Part III introduces a third setting for the action of the novel: the river Scamander on the plain of Troy. While the river bank is an attractive place to rest, the travellers later move into a rural area destroyed by war (p.155). Lighter moments – such as Priam and Somax bathing their feet and eating together in a pleasant pastoral setting – are countered by this sombre scene, reminding the reader of the cost to everyone of long years of conflict. As the journey progresses, Somax comes to regard Priam as being like a child who does not know much about everyday life (p.115) whilst Priam appreciates Somax's courtesy and consideration for his well-being (p.125). The brave persistence needed by a character such as Somax to get through life's challenges is celebrated. He may not be a famous warrior but he shows heroism of another kind in dealing with severe difficulties and the loss of loved ones. The reader might compare his fortitude with the extreme behaviour of Achilles in Part I and Priam in Part II.

The important theme of storytelling is developed. Priam realises that the way Somax talks freely about his life opens a fresh way of experiencing the world. It is interesting and exciting to Priam (p.128). When Hermes appears disguised as a young man but is revealed to be a god, it is the conventions of storytelling which allow the real world and fantasy to acceptably combine. Hermes labels Somax 'a storyteller and spinner of tales' (p.157). He likes to chatter and hear news of the world around him (p.158), as expected of a divine messenger, but he is also the god of heralds. Somax, as the new Idaeus, is thus unexpectedly linked with Hermes' role. As we learn in Part V, Somax will continue to spin yarns about his adventures with Priam for the rest of his long life.

Knowing that he is approaching a great challenge, Priam feels strengthened by Somax's presence, an unusual meeting of the 'higher' and 'lower' orders of Troy. He recognises that Somax's approach to experience contrasts with his own which relies on predictable ceremonies and customs. Somax interprets his life story as one of 'endless surprise and accident' (p.161) so he is able to deal calmly even with a god's arrival. That Hermes' visit is a surprise and the cart narrowly escapes

Hermes, messenger of the gods

collapsing into the river works in two ways: these events advance the plot but are also signs to the reader that storytelling is a focus here.

Key point

Priam's power as king partly comes from his careful use of words and silence. His speech contrasts with the freer, down-to-earth language of Somax: 'In [Priam's] own world a man spoke only to give shape to a decision he had come to, or to lay out an argument for or against ... To pay a compliment whose decorative phrases, and appeals to vanity or family pride, were fixed and of ancient and approved form. Silence, not speech, was what was expressive. Power lay in containment' (p.126). In Priam's view, Somax is what he would never want to be: a 'chatterer' (p.125) but the carter's free-flowing talk accords with 'a prattling world' (p.126). Priam hears that all of nature has a 'low, continuous rustling and buzzing and humming' (p.127). Perhaps, Priam realises, there is another kind of power other than human force, one more closely connected to the living earth. Its language values all of life, no matter how small or seemingly unimportant.

Q The narrative shifts viewpoint regularly in Part III so that the reader sees events through Somax's eyes as well as through Priam's. What do you think is achieved by this?

Q 'The appearance of Hermes is pure fantasy.' Is Hermes too much for the reader to believe in? Explain your view of Hermes' role in Part III.

Part IV (pp.167–201)

Summary: *Achilles is surprised when Priam announces he has brought a ransom for his son's body. Priam's appeal moves Achilles to agree to his request. After looking once more at Hector's body, Achilles feels freed from his oppressive sorrow.*

Achilles sits in the mess hut with his men and his attendants, Automedon and Alcimus (p.167). He feels depressed and eats little. The noisy comradeship of the men and their physical strength are highlighted (p.168). The reliable Automedon has replaced Patroclus as Achilles' chief attendant. He loves

Achilles and is concerned about his well-being, though hurt by his resentment. It was Automedon who held the dying Patroclus and fought off the Trojans, something that arouses Achilles' jealousy (p.169).

An element of fantasy enters the story again as 'a hand sweeps across sounding strings' (p.171). The music of the lyre alters Achilles' mood, opening his mind to the fluid world of his mother, Thetis. His 'hard, manly qualities' are softened by the feminine influence of the goddess (p.172). He apprehends (senses, feels) in a way that reminds the reader of Priam's vision of the goddess Iris in Part II. Both men have the facility of mind to be in contact with higher influences. Achilles sees a vague figure – is it Patroclus or perhaps his father Peleus? The memory of his father's love fills 'the great Achilles' with tenderness and tears (p.174). In a gesture that is opposite to this episode in Homer's *Iliad*, Achilles kneels before Priam, showing how much he values the father-son relationship. Even though he sees his mistake as the aged Priam reveals his true identity, Achilles stays open to a moment of emotion he rarely shows others. He senses unusual influences at work that change his reactions (p.175).

After Priam explains his mission and that he has been 'guided', Achilles understands the gods are favouring Priam's request (p.176). Somax has difficulty explaining his position as 'Idaeus' but Priam's elegant and gracious speech expresses Somax's value to him (p.181). Formal speech, too, has a place when dealing with powerful people like Achilles. When Priam begs Achilles as one father to another to release Hector's body, the warrior is surprised and moved, as he has suppressed his feelings about his own son (Neoptolemus) for a long time (p.183). Priam appeals to their common humanity and sense of honour (pp.182–83). The look on Achilles' face fills Priam with compassion and he kneels before him (p.187), as he expected to do in the first place. Achilles shows new understanding as he agrees to give back Hector's body and offers Priam his hand to help him stand. This physical gesture of reconciliation, further developed as they eat together (pp.197–99), is a key moment for Achilles in the novel (p.187).

When Achilles views Hector's body one last time, he understands that he is finally free from grief. His heart has been cleared like the air around him (p.190). He can regard Hector as a warrior who has won an honourable death and accepts his own death to come. He has been given time to learn, to find 'the true Achilles' (p.190) with the gods' favour. He now sees that compassion towards his enemy can be a strength and not a weakness.

He visits the hut where women are preparing to wash Hector's body, a place he would not usually enter. He recalls the role of women in his society during birth and childhood ('the first world we come into', p.193) and then in a warrior's burial. Achilles seems at home now in the company of fellow warriors, his Myrmidons, with their 'bodies sinewy, taut, ready for hard use' (p.193). He has chosen his role rather than just accepted his fate.

Under Achilles' protection, Priam sleeps safely in the enemy camp and then prepares to travel back to Troy. As he awakes, the change in his way of seeing the world is highlighted. He has a 'new-found eye for ... irrelevant happenings' (p.195) that lends him fresh energy for the day ahead. He is curious to know Achilles better and is again startled by his physical strength and his 'horrible potential' to kill in battle (p.197). If he and Achilles valued more their common humanity perhaps the war might be 'otherwise' (p.197) and end differently. They part knowing that violent deaths await them. The future has shown itself in visions and has been accepted, as in a traditional epic: they are 'smiling in the foreknowledge of what they have already seen' (p.201), a passivity that may seem strange to the modern reader but fitting to the period of Homer.

The narrative structure of Part IV makes use of shifts in time to achieve a flow between past, present and future. There is immediate action (pp.175–76, for example), summary of memories (pp.173–74), flashback (p.183) and flash-forward (p.186). After the music of the lyre sounds (p.172), a quieter tone suspends the noise of the men in the hut. The main characters seem caught up in a kind of slow motion. Time becomes the setting of the novel, more than place, as Achilles observes in Part I.

Achilles' point of view blends with that of the third person narrator for most of Part IV, although Priam's view of Achilles is also important. His frailty highlights Achilles' physical strength. Priam's ability to speak well becomes a strength he can use to further his cause. The gesture of kneeling signals that both men are open to feeling for the other. Part IV has a strong, dramatic quality suitable for the climax of the novel.

Key point

The nature of being human is highlighted in Part IV. Are the characters ruled by animal instincts, by the influence of the gods or by human reason and feelings? A blend of all these facets suggests the permeable, open nature of human beings in the novel. Achilles, for example, admires the 'overabundance ... of an animal nature' in the young Alcimus, a force he will need to 'subdue' in maturity. Priam reminds Achilles of the importance of family affections. They are both fathers and sons before anything else: each is a 'poor mortal' destined to die (p.182). Priam begs Achilles to accept the ransom for Hector, showing that 'we are men, children of the gods, not raving beasts' (p.183). The value of making ethical choices is highlighted here. The novel puts forward the view that humans should show mercy and kindness to each other, even though these high ideals are constantly compromised by human aggression. 'What does it mean to be human?' is a question the novel poses, using the past as a mirror for current dilemmas.

Q How is Achilles persuaded to return Hector's body? Is it only Priam's words that make him change his mind?

Q 'Even though Priam and Achilles part with greater respect for each other, the war will still go on.' Does the novel offer only limited hope? Discuss your view.

Q 'Power belongs to the strong.' Does it? Does the 'feminine' have any power in this predominantly 'masculine' realm? How are power and strength represented in Part IV?

Part V (pp.205–19) and 'Afterword' (pp.221–24)

Summary: *Priam travels home, bringing the body of Hector back to Troy.*

It is a homecoming with touches of comedy and tragedy for Priam: his joy at regaining Hector's body from the enemy is mixed with his knowledge of Troy's future destruction and his own violent death. Priam has regained his sense of self-worth and confidence. He tries to suppress his fears, telling himself that he is 'coming home to a state of exultant wellbeing in which he ... is divinely led as by music' (p.211). Thanks to Somax, he has gained a freer way of behaving and feeling.

Achilles is confident too and glad to feel whole again. He is full of high spirits as he prepares his sword for battle. While the future seems suspended (p.211), the chorus-like narrative (as in a Greek tragedy) relates through a dramatic flash-forward sequence (pp.212–14) how fate will take its course (p.212). Killing and revenge will trouble the life of his son, Neoptolemus, whose shame at slaughtering Priam so mercilessly shows the warrior ideal as a heavy burden, a problematic legacy passed from father to son. Not every fight will lead to enduring tales of 'glory'.

Somax lives on among the lower orders of society in a world somewhat apart from the tragic realm of the heroic characters. His role as a storyteller is emphasised, an early forerunner, perhaps, of epic poets like Homer. The ideas expressed about storytelling are light-hearted yet thought-provoking. Where does truth begin and end in what is termed 'history'? In what sense might myths be 'true'? Why have they been so highly valued? The final image is of the mule Beauty, suggesting that one story can lead to another, then to legends as events in the present recede far into the past. In this sense, it is a happy ending. The human love of stories is emphasised and valued highly.

Key point

The evocative description of the war-torn landscape (pp.205–206) ensures that Priam's homecoming is not one of simple joy even though he feels: 'This is triumph' (p.208). The women in the field give a further role to the feminine in the novel as they 'move close to the earth, their hands turning the clods, breaking them with practised fingers' (p.206). Survival is the focus of the common people and puts Priam's personal triumph in perspective.

Q Priam believes he is 'coming home, even in these last days of his life, as a man remade' (p.209). What does he mean by this? Should he be more concerned about the war that will recommence after the truce?

Q 'The life of Somax seems to end more happily than the other characters.' Why do you think the novel ends by focusing on Somax and the mule Beauty? Is this a satisfying conclusion for the reader?

CHARACTERS & RELATIONSHIPS

Achilles

Key quotes

'The man is a fighter, but when he is not fighting he is a farmer, earth is his element.' (p.4)

'For the whole of his life he has been drawn, in his other nature, to his mother's element. To what, in all its many forms, as ocean, pool, stream, is shifting and insubstantial.' (p.4)

'What he feels in himself as a perfect order of body, heart, occasion, is the enactment, under the stars, in the very breath of the gods, of the true Achilles, the one he has come all this way to find.' (p.190)

Achilles' killing of Hector, followed by the defiling of his body, are the overall catalysts for the action. His inner quest to find 'the true Achilles' (p.190) is central to the plot, although at first it seems that the death of his close companion Patroclus is what drives him. Achilles' crisis of identity as a hero and the way he resolves it (pp.187–90) gives the reader an intimate view of a complex personality.

The narrative blends a third-person view with a perspective that is often seen through Achilles' eyes. A tough fighter with great physical strength, Achilles has a sensitive side that is presented to the reader from the opening paragraph as he listens for his mother's voice. Like Priam, Achilles knows when a god is communicating with him. In Part I the reader gets to know Achilles in a way that others do not and carries this knowledge forward as the narrative develops so contrasting views of him can be compared. Our sympathy for Achilles is in some ways surprising, given his role as a brutal, determined killer. Hecuba's description of him as a 'jackal, that noble bully' (p.57) applies a predator-like image to Achilles that is repeated in Priam's view of his 'animal eyes' (p.197). Priam also finds 'the whole terrible machinery of the man' (p.199) fearful. Force is part of Achilles' very being and physique. We are told he is a farmer when he is not fighting (p.4) but he is never shown in this more peaceful role.

It is Achilles' decision to release Hector's body and accept his role as a hero-warrior that brings him peace in Part IV. This is again described in Part V where Achilles is 'visited by a lightness that is both new and a return' (p.211). His body feels again 'the dance of blood' and his heels (the mortal part of him) glow. His confidence is supreme yet immediately challenged in the narrative by the dramatic account of his son mercilessly slaughtering Priam. It is as if Achilles has a premonition (a vision ahead of time) of the burden of revenge that he will leave to Neoptolemus.

Key points

Achilles' personality is influenced by his origins, expressed in his love for his father Peleus (mortal, of the earth) and his mother Thetis (immortal, of water). The feminine influence (described as fluid) has declined, however, as he has become a hardened fighter who needs to release his suppressed emotions of grief and anger to be restored to harmony within himself. His focus is the world of fighting men.

The nature of Achilles' heroism is an important aspect of his dilemma. He has seen Patroclus act out the hero-warrior's death while pretending to be Achilles. Now he has killed Hector and defiled his body in rage. Is being a famous hero-warrior a sort of play-acting? Will Achilles waste his life in an early death? Like Hector's, his name will live on in legend as long as stories are told, the kind of immortality that the ancient world of epic poems valued most highly. What is he achieving, especially given the burden of revenge that Neoptolemus must carry? We see the civilians near Troy who are battered by war. Their lives question the value of war and violence in the novel and, by implication, the ethic of the traditional warrior-hero.

Priam

Key quotes

'My role was to hold myself apart in ceremonial stillness and let others be my arm, my fist – my breath too when talk was needed ... I have always had a herald.' (p.53)

'It seems to me ... that there might be another way of naming what we call fortune ... or the whim of the gods. Which offers a kind of opening. The opportunity to act for ourselves. To try something that might force events into a different course.' (p.61)

> 'Achilles ... we are mortals, not gods. We die. Death is in our nature ... we should have pity for one another's losses ... [I come] a plain man white-haired and old, and entreat the killer of [my] son ... to remember his own death, and the death of his father, and do as these things are honourably done among us, to take the ransom I bring and give me back my son.' (pp.184–85)

Priam shares the central position with Achilles when they meet at the climax of the novel. He is the opposite of Achilles in age, physical strength and role. Priam has a passive, ceremonial role as king, whereas Achilles' life is dominated by action. Priam relies on long-held traditions and on formal, courteous, graceful language to exert his power. He always behaves as he believes a king should. His wife Hecuba and all those around him expect him to act predictably; they are shocked when he announces that he plans to try something different in going to Achilles as just a man rather than as a king. His relationship with Hecuba is important as it is his wife he must try to convince about his plans for the ransom. Their long, loving and intimate relationship shows a gentle, loyal side of Priam. Despite their disagreement about his plans, he is excited to see Hecuba waiting for him on the walls of Troy as he returns (p.215).

Priam has become used to other people doing things for him, including the herald Idaeus who speaks for him at public occasions. Priam's decision to travel with the carter Somax has a positive result in this area of his life. Somax coaxes Prim to rest, bathe his feet in the river and eat simple food. He even explains how pikelets are made. Priam recognises that he knows nothing about the way things are put together and that there is much more to the world than he thought. By talking with Somax, Priam hears about the challenges of a life other than his own. Although Somax is from the lower orders of Trojan society, he has experienced deep grief over the death of his wife and children. Priam discovers a new-found curiosity in what he had formerly regarded as irrelevant to his life.

Priam comes to value his role as a father during his ransom quest, prompted by his genuine love for Hector. When Hermes calls him 'father' (p.161) Priam realises he is about to act as a 'father' before Achilles in a new, demanding way. Achilles, too, calls Priam 'father' (p.174) thinking, at first, that he is Peleus. When Neoptolemus also speaks the word 'father' as he kills Priam to avenge Achilles' death (a flash-forward sequence, p.213), the old king 'turns upon him a ghastly far-off smile' as if recalling the earlier occasions when he was called by that title. It is not just as a king that he will die but as a father who has come to appreciate that role, its joys, loyalties and burdens.

Priam's humility and dignity are made clear when he speaks with Achilles. He is a noble leader, even though he says he is coming as just a man (p.184). Achilles respects his dignified and gracious behaviour. Priam's appeal to their shared mortality and their roles as fathers points to significant ethical values in the novel. Priam values family affections and loyalty. He forgives his enemy and takes a chance to break the deadlock. This is still the world of the classical Greek epic, however, and 'taking a chance' is given certain limits in the novel out of respect for Homer's worldview in *The Iliad*. Like Achilles, Priam accepts that war will resume after the truce and that he will die when Troy falls. He accepts fate but has been transformed by his efforts to move events in a positive direction. His deep feeling of unworthiness, drawn from his childhood memories (p.68), is balanced by a sense of achievement and triumph (p.208). He is now truly 'Priam', the ransomed one. Authentic identity and self-worth have been personal goals for Priam and Achilles in the novel.

The reader sees resilience, determination and self-control at work in Priam's personality. The boundaries of the classical epic are stretched by the main characters' choices and complex personalities.

Key points

Priam is glad that he has achieved something for which he will be remembered other than his impending violent death. He has won back Hector's body and can bury it properly. Initiative and tradition have both motivated his actions. He will have a place in stories, as he desires. Priam has 'stepped into a space that till now was uninhabited and found a way to fill it' (p.208).

The peace of mind Priam feels is notable in Part V. He accepts that 'one day then the next; no more than that can be counted on. But in his present mood it is enough' (p.209). He is 'coming home to a state of exultant well-being in which he ... is divinely led as by music' (p.211), an image that reminds the reader of the sound of the lyre (p.172) which opened Achilles' mind to a better way of thinking and feeling.

Somax

Key quotes

'His name is Somax. It fits him, he has always thought, rather well. He has been comfortable with it, warm and very much himself, for a good fifty years, give or take a few.' (p.98)

'He steadies himself by turning to his mules, who stand patient amid so much fluster, waiting for him.' (p.100)

Somax 'straightened and turned back to where Priam, looking uncertain and out of place, stood watching. He's like a child, he thought, a bit on the slow side.' (p.115)

Somax is the third main character in the novel. His presence brings a lighter, sometimes comic tone to the narrative (his view of the chickenhawk, for example, on p.101) which balances the darker tone of Part I and the beginning of Part II. Somax's life in the lower orders of Trojan society contrasts with the formal, ritualised practices of the king's citadel and the war-focused activity of Achilles' camp. Unlike Achilles and Priam, Somax is content with his identity (p.98) and is reluctant to have the name of 'Idaeus' placed upon him by the princes of Troy. He sees Priam as a child (p.115) who has little skill in managing daily life, a view that places Priam in a kind, yet humorous light on the serious journey they are undertaking. Somax's distrust of Hermes when he appears creates an ironic comic interlude between the two characters. Priam quickly learns to respect and value Somax for his common sense, kindness and loyalty. Somax's character does not develop as fully as Priam's and Achilles' but his reliable good humour, self-awareness and resilience in dealing with life's good and bad times are notable qualities. Like the mules that steady Somax when he feels uncertain (p.100), his down-to-earth language balances the abstract speech of Priam. His enjoyment of daily life motivates Priam to try to think the same way.

Somax's affection for his mules brings rural harmony to the novel, as in a pastoral scene. He is especially fond of Beauty and knows that it was her attractiveness and intelligence that caused him to be chosen as Priam's companion. He feels comforted when he sees her 'round eye, its clear glistening white' (p.207). Somax is a sympathetic character who adds interest and depth to the novel. He is a spinner of yarns himself; as he grows old his listeners cannot believe that what he describes is not legend (or a lie) rather than a story of events that actually happened to him. This suggests that Somax can be seen as an early forerunner of Homer himself.

Key points

Somax's love for his family causes Priam to reassess the way he relates to his own children. As Somax returns to Troy he thinks 'with a burst of joy' of his little grand-daughter. His daughter-in-law's skill in making pikelets catches Priam's imagination, an example of the small details of Somax's life which have a large impact on the king. The story implies that the lower orders of society have something to teach to the higher.

At the end of Part V, his disbelieving listeners view Somax as 'this old fellow [who], like most storytellers, is a stealer of other men's tales, of other men's lives' (p.218). They think Somax is making up tales about helping the king and meeting the great Achilles. The reader, however, knows that he is telling the truth.

Hecuba

Key quotes

'They sit a moment, holding one another like children. The lamp flickers. She weeps. When her tears have come to an end, and she has once again taken control of herself, he begins.' (p.50)

'I carried him,' she whispers, 'here, here,' and her clenched fist beats at the hollow under her heart. 'It is *my* flesh that is being tumbled on the stones out there.' (p.52)

Hecuba, Priam's wife, is the principal female character. She shows determination and self-control in all of her actions. Her conversation with Priam in Part II is an important occasion not so much for what it reveals about her but for the opportunity it provides for Priam to talk about his plans and early life. She is used to dealing with Priam's dreams (p.55). Her strong feelings as a mother are evident as she thinks about what has happened to Hector's body (p.52). Her relations with her children seem closer than Priam's and point to his lack of real connection with many in his family. Hecuba believes in following the traditional ways and is understandably shocked by Priam's plan to ransom Hector's body. She can be persuasive and very influential at gatherings of the Trojan court (pp.80–81). By taking charge at the ceremony that seeks the gods blessing before Priam departs (p.101), Hecuba shows that she knows the limits of her power as well as her duty. She prompts the priest Helenus to proclaim that an eagle can be seen in the sky, a sign of Jove's favour. That Somax thinks it is a chickenhawk counters the abstract faith of the courtiers but does not detract from their ideal of harmony between humans and gods.

Patroclus

Key quotes

'The boy Patroclus tilts his chin, thin brows drawn in expectation ... and for the first time Achilles meets his gaze. Patroclus looks at him. The blow connects, bone on bone. And the boy, his clear eyes still fixed on Achilles, takes it.' (p.13)

'Out there on the glittering plain, a figure dressed like him and moving as he did, resplendent in his harness, breastplate and greaves and holding aloft his studded shield, was standing alone between the lines.' (p.19)

Achilles is haunted by the memory of Patroclus: his ghost appears once to request that his body be buried (p.20) and he thinks he might be approaching as Priam enters the hut (p.172). Patroclus' death underscores Achilles' torment, grief and confusion throughout the novel. As boys, they grew up together after Patroclus was taken in by Peleus. Both their lives seem bound up with early death – the accidental killing by Patroclus of his playfellow, his own death at the hands of Hector and Achilles' death soon to come. Patroclus is like a 'shadow' of Achilles, although he is aware that he is not Achilles' equal (p.14). Patroclus feels desperate when Achilles withdraws from battle. He values the warrior's code of honour very highly and risks his life to bring his own version of Achilles back into the war. He cannot match Hector and his death is predictable, if shocking, to everyone when his true identity is revealed. In wearing Achilles' armour he has brought into question the unique identity of the hero. Was Patroclus wrong to believe in the ideal of honour in battle? Achilles must deal with the fact that Patroclus' love for him led to his terrible slaughter.

Hector

Key quotes

'The armour Hector wore was the armour he had stripped from the body of Patroclus, Achilles' own, which Hector wore now to mock him.' (pp.22–3)

'He spoke to Achilles with the last of his breath; as men, both, for whom this moment was sacred; a meeting that from the beginning had been the clear goal of their lives and the final achievement of what they were. Man to man, but impersonally.' (p.23)

The horror at Achilles' treatment of Hector's body motivates Priam to attempt to retrieve him for traditional burial. Hector is a brave and skilful fighter whose death signals the coming destruction of Troy, as he was the city's main protector. As he dies, Hector speaks to Achilles without hatred (p.23), demonstrating the value he places on the warrior ideal. Hector and Achilles believed that the soul would travel to the underworld (p.25) and have an afterlife there. To live on in legend was another form of 'afterlife' that such heroes desired.

By the end of *Ransom*, Hector's ideals are finally honoured by Achilles (p.190). Looking at his corpse, he admires the 'clean-limbed perfection of it, the splendour of the warrior who has won an honourable death' and it was 'no longer an affront' (p.190). Achilles understands that, like Patroclus, the gods have given Hector an important place in his own life and destiny. Achilles 'can now take [Hector's honour in death] as an honour intended also to himself' (p.190). Malouf acknowledges the values of the epic in this regard, while Neoptolemus' butchery of Priam (pp.212–14) shows the reverse side of the warrior's code.

Hermes

Key quotes

'Leaning in a leisurely manner against the rails of the wagon, right foot crossed elegantly on the left, was a slim youth in a winged bonnet, below which his hair, which was of a burnished golden-bronze, hung in glossy ringlets.' (p.143)

'The youth – Hermes – clasped his wrist and Priam felt a jolt as his blood responded to the firm, rather icy touch. Then a slow energy flooded his limbs.' (p.161)

The god Hermes is introduced as an embodiment of the fantastic, strange and marvellous in the narrative. He belongs to myth and legend, though placed here in what seems a 'realistic' world to stretch the boundaries of the genre. Is this a mythical tale, a romantic quest or an epic? It has elements of all these forms. Hermes' presence is a playful way of encouraging the reader to think about what stories are and what makes them appealing. As we might expect, a down-to-earth character like Somax finds Hermes a nuisance, as would readers who prefer a realistic story. Priam, given to airy dreams and 'jelly-like' visions (p.41), recognises who Hermes is and welcomes his presence, as a reader who likes fantasy might do also.

Hermes has a mischievous and clever nature that is revealed easily through his disguise as Orchilus, one of Achilles' men (p.145). He was credited in ancient times with a number of roles that are relevant to events and characters in *Ransom*. He is the god of heralds and communication, 'the celestial joker – messenger, thief, trickster, escort of souls to the underworld' (p.159). Hermes favours Priam's quest and his interactions with the travellers are positive. The gods are not always on the side of Troy: Priam observes that 'the gods are not to be trusted when they tilt the balance momentarily in your favour' (p.208).

THEMES, IDEAS & VALUES

Taking a chance – choosing action

Key quotes

'Not a mockery, my friend, but the way things *are*. Not the way they must be, but the way they have turned out. In a world that is also subject to chance.' (Iris to Priam, p.46)

'[Priam] has stepped into a space that till now was uninhabited and found a way to fill it. Not as he filled his old role as king, since all he had to do was follow convention, slip his arms into the sleeves of an empty garment and stand still, but as one for whom every gesture had still to be hit upon, every word discovered anew …' (pp.208–209)

Priam acts in an unexpected way to achieve a positive goal when he decides to follow chance rather than passive customs. In doing so he must oppose those close to him who expect the king to always be predictable. He feels 'bold' and 'defiant' (p.49). Priam's appearance in the invaders' camp as a simple man in a simple cart also frees Achilles from his torment and grief. They both find another way to be themselves. Achilles honours Hector's death, as the ideals of the classical world require, and in doing so honours his own death. Priam rids himself of his lifelong feeling of inadequacy in his role as king. His lack of confidence started in childhood when he was briefly cast into slavery before being ransomed by his sister, Hesione. She took a chance to save Priam and it worked. The gods favour Priam's decision to redeem Hector's body and support him along the way.

The novel brings together potentially conflicting ideas about why things happen, blending classical Greek thinking with modern ideas. The concept that humans have free will to act and should take opportunities as they come was foreign to the ancient Greeks, who believed that human life is governed by larger powers such as a greater destiny or supernatural beings. The narrative allows each of these approaches to work in the story. We see some of the characters decide to risk action and take a chance, yet they still accept the workings of fate and the interference of the gods.

Key points

The novel invites us to ask questions about our own beliefs. Should we believe in fate or chance? How should a person decide?

The novel implies that people's actions are influenced by what is thought possible at any moment in history. What are some current limits on our ways of thinking about an important problem? What new idea might cause a breakthrough? Where might that idea come from?

Pity and compassion

Key quotes

'Death is in our nature. Without that fee paid in advance, the world does not come to us. That is ... the condition we share. And for that reason, if for no other, we should have pity for one another's losses. For the sorrows that must come ... in a world we enter only on mortal terms.' (Priam to Achilles, p.184)

'It does high honour to both of us ... to show that we are men, children of the gods, not ravening beasts'. (Priam to Achilles, p.183)

'At [Achilles'] feet, the body whose quiet he can accept now as a mirror of his own. So long as he sits here, there can be no conflict between them. They are in perfect amity. Their part in the long war is at an end.' (Achilles with Hector's body, p.191)

Even in the long, harsh war between the Trojans and Greeks, enduring human values emerge. Priam, dressed simply and with no weapons or crown, pleads with Achilles to release Hector's body. He appeals to his humanity and in doing so raises the question of what it means to be 'human'. Does being human mean that there are responsibilities everyone must take on? Should humans have a basic respect for each other and show compassion? What is the basis for such values? What beliefs do they imply?

Both Priam and Achilles come to a new understanding of what it means to be human. For just over a day Priam ceases to be a king and lives as a man, sharing simple pleasures with Somax on the journey and humbling himself before Achilles out of love for his son. He pleads with Achilles as one human to another. Since we all die in the end, he argues, we should feel each other's sorrows now and be compassionate. Achilles' decision to respect Hector's body and accept the ransom shows that he is ruled by honour rather than by basic animal instincts. He contemplates Hector's body and his own death with fresh respect. In pitying Priam as a father, Achilles is reminded of his own son Neoptolemus and changes his view of Hector. This brings him into 'perfect amity' (p.191) or friendship with someone he saw before as his 'implacable enemy' (p.10).

Key point

Compassion and kindness appear in everyday moments as well as dramatic events: Somax is kind to Priam as they travel; he looks after his precious mules; Somax's son arranged the cooking stones to assist his wife in preparing food for the family (p.119). The value of compassion goes beyond social class and political beliefs.

Gender roles and power

Key quotes

'The man [Achilles] is a fighter, but when he is not fighting he is a farmer, earth is his element.' (p.4)

'But the look [Hecuba] casts upon him is so fierce that he draws back and cannot go on. He feels the hard purpose he has come with flutter in him and fail.' (p.51)

'[Achilles] has moved into his mother's element and is open again to her shimmering influence. In such moods he *sees things* …' (p.172)

'Till [Achilles] too, like Hector, is in there. Naked as he began. Being turned this way and that in the hands of women.' (p.194)

The novel is set in a world where political power belongs predominantly to men. While he is exceptional in his physical power and skills, Achilles is described as a 'fighter' or a 'farmer' (p.4); roles which require hard, physical work. Like his Myrmidons, Hector, Patroclus and the armies of both sides, the role of the warrior is a key aspect of men's identity at this time. Somax represents an alternative male role. As a carter, he is a service provider, involved in taking goods from one place to another each day, managing animals and goods in commerce. Priam, a king, is in a unique position of high authority. His power comes from fulfilling traditional expectations and making wise decisions that sustain Troy's civilisation.

The role of women in *Ransom* is far more limited. Hecuba and her daughters have positions of social privilege in the Trojan court. Her position as Priam's first and favourite wife means that others try to gain her favour (p.80). Priam wants her approval because he respects and loves her. Although Hecuba intimidates him (p.51), he defies her wishes in going to Achilles' camp, proving her authority is limited. In classical mythology, the prophetess Cassandra has the ability to see the future but no one will ever believe her. In *Ransom* she has very little influence and is regarded by Priam and the family as 'overwrought' (p.42).

Female figures have significant power in the myths and legends that the novel draws upon. The goddesses Iris and Thetis influence Priam and Achilles respectively. Achilles' mother, who is present as a feminine influence rather than a personality, is very important to him. Thetis is associated with the energy of flowing water (p.4), with sexual fertility and the motion of atoms which make up matter. The novel represents as 'feminine' those underlying forces that are always at work in the very fabric of life, as distinct from the biological 'female' identity of characters. Achilles apprehends solid forms becoming particles that 'tumble and swarm' (p.172). Priam too is transformed as he becomes more alert to the ever-shifting energies of nature (p.114) and the little details of daily life during his journey with Somax. He notices for the first time the endless sounds of a 'prattling' natural world (p.126). Both Achilles and Priam benefit from allowing 'feminine' aspects of their personalities to have more influence so that they can balance their exualted roles with a fuller, more even form of humanity.

The view of the 'female' and 'feminine' is complex in the novel and should not be over-simplified. There are key episodes that bring local women into the story but they tend to perform set tasks. Somax's daughter-in-law and young grand-daughter feature in his conversations with Priam but they are never referred to by their names. They seem emblematic of people in everyday life rather than individuals in their own right. They perhaps belong to the 'spaces' in another story, in the same way that Somax has entered this one. Local women from Achilles' camp are given narrative time in Part IV. Achilles connects their hands that turn Hector's body 'this way and that' (p.194) with rituals of birth and death. He is fascinated by the work they will carry out on Hector's corpse. As traditional male and female gendered roles in society can enhance or suppress human potential, so assigning terms such as 'masculine' and 'feminine' to ways of perceiving the world can risk over-categorising individual differences. The novel treads a careful path in this much-discussed area of human experience.

Key point

Political and social power in the novel is predominantly masculine. This fits the world of Homer's epic but images in the novel show that a balance between 'masculine' and 'feminine' qualities of perception is valued.

The important influence of the goddesses Iris and Thetis points to a psychological and mythical power that the novel associates with the feminine.

Storytelling

Key quotes

'It was as if you found yourself peering through the crack in a door (exciting, Priam found, this imagining himself into a situation he would never have dreamed of acting out …' (p.127)

'He was enjoying it ... already telling himself, in his head, the story of their crossing and feeling steadfast, even bold.' (p.153)

'So many stories! He tells them to anyone who will share a drink with him ... This old fellow, like most storytellers, is a stealer of other men's tales, of other men's lives.' (pp.218–19)

The nature of stories is an important theme in the novel. In Part III, Priam shows a new interest in events around him and this curiosity is the basic state of mind needed for telling and listening to stories. Rather than an epic tragedy, the story takes on qualities of an adventure tale, drawing features from all kinds of storytelling traditions. Priam enjoys the sensation that he too is in a story that is unfolding.

Somax, identified by Hermes as a 'spinner of yarns' (p.157), is given considerable narrative time to tell us about his life (pp.130–34) in plain, yet engaging language. While his world contrasts with that of Priam, they share the loss of children. Through Somax's narrative Priam reflects on his own experience. Having realised that being a king has distanced him emotionally, he starts to seek a stronger connection with his surroundings.

The relationship between stories, history and myths is suggested in the closing pages of the novel, which focus on the role of Somax. His listeners come to regard him as a drunken old liar. His mule Beauty is more interesting and 'real' in their memories than anything Somax has to say. She, no doubt, will become part of future stories. Somax, the reader knows, has in fact experienced the events of his tales but as time goes on memory and imagination inevitably blend. What is fact and what is fiction? Told in a future where Troy is only a memory, Somax's stories highlight the value of putting into words what experience brings us so richly every day. By revisiting past stories, we enrich the present and imagine the future. Stories are an essential part of who we are, the novel shows, as it gives fresh life to 'crevices' found in Homer's ancient tale.

Key points

Somax is important in showing how stories come from both good and bad times in everyday life. He 'heralds' to Priam that life in all its little details and range of emotions is of great interest.

Malouf plays with ideas of what a novel can do as opposed to a traditional epic. This includes freedom to bring in characters from all levels of society, explore emotions in depth, introduce episodes that might at first seem irrelevant and value individual uniqueness rather than people playing set roles. The novelist takes a chance, as does Priam.

Family ties and friendships

Key quotes

'He knew every movement of Patroclus' soul – how could he not after so long? – but would not allow himself to be swayed.' (p.16)

'I shook all over. I thought, "I can't bear it, if anything happens to this little one, the last of my blood." I don't know what I'd have done if the gods hadn't thought again and been kind to us.' (Somax, p.131)

'Think, Achilles. Think of your son, Neoptolemus. Would you not do for him what I am doing here for Hector? Would your father, Peleus, not do the same for you?' (p.184)

Affection for family and friends is a central value in the novel, as in human societies throughout time. The expectation that family members will be loyal to each other and even fight for each other was a basic belief in Homer's epic world, although betrayal, family murders and revenge were ever-present. The Trojan War and its aftermath show such values at work.

The novel contrasts the sometimes distant feeling that Priam has for his children with the love that Somax feels for his offspring. Priam has lost dozens of sons 'all of them dear to him – or so he had told himself' (p.135). He lives a life of ritual rather than true affection. Only his son Hector's defilement by Achilles stirs him to act. When asking for Hector's body, Priam appeals to Achilles to remember his love for his son, Neoptolemus, and Peleus' love for him. Love for family is right at the centre of both men's actions and values. In this way, all characters suffer equally from the destruction of war. Loss, not joy, is their common experience.

Although Part V shows Priam and Somax rejoicing at the prospect of going home and being reunited with their loved ones, the war will resume and more deaths will come. What is more important – being with your loved ones or fighting a war? Achilles in particular must make this choice. He is not fighting to defend his family – his need is to be a hero, to win fame and glory. He knows, however, that there will be a high cost for his son who will come to Troy to avenge Achilles' death. In grieving so deeply for his close companion Patroclus, Achilles is possibly expressing his own grief and anger at the choices he has made and the worldview he is caught up in.

Key point

Close male friendships and father-son loyalties are important in the novel. Family loyalties can test the values of characters. Priam must defy his family to go on the journey he believes he needs to make. Achilles chooses to stay at Troy rather than go home, even though Priam reminds him that he has a family: the values of the warrior-hero are more important to him.

"The Destruction Of Troy" from the fresco by Peter Von Cornelius (1787–1867)

DIFFERENT INTERPRETATIONS

Different interpretations arise from different responses to a text. Over time, a text will give rise to a wide range of responses from its readers, who may come from various social or cultural groups and live in very different places and historical periods. Theses responses can be published in newspapers, journals and books by critics and reviewers, or they can be expressed in discussion among readers in the media, classrooms, book groups and so on. While there is no single correct reading or interpretation of a text, it is important to understand that an interpretation is more than a personal opinion – it is the justification of a point of view on the text. To present an interpretation of the text based on your point of view you must use a logical argument and support it with relevant evidence from the text.

The critics' viewpoints

Since its publication in 2009, *Ransom* has been extensively reviewed both in Australia and internationally. Typical of the many favourable views of the book is Coates' comment 'that this tender novel lingers so long and hauntingly in the mind is a testament both to Malouf's poetry and to his reverence for the endless power of myth' (*Sunday Book Review*). Other critics describe it as 'pithy and wise' (Manguel, *Australian Literary Review*) and 'Shakespearean [in] those quiet moments when time stands still and the nature of life is mysteriously revealed' (Riemer, *Sydney Morning Herald*). Critics have particularly praised the high quality of Malouf's prose: 'vivid and often wonderfully detailed ... the prose is specific and noble' (White, *Books of the Times*); Malouf 'embroiders [his paraphrase] with imaginative details that often reanimate familiar elements of the epic' (Mendelsohn, *New Yorker*). Others prefer the 'terror' and 'astonishing gore' of Homer, finding some of Malouf's characterisation of Achilles rather passive and lacking in action when compared to Homer's version (Rose, *Australian Book Review*).

Critics have differed in their opinions of the way Malouf uses the *The Iliad* as the basis of *Ransom*. Those who prefer a close adaptation of Homer's original see the idea of 'chance' Malouf gives to Priam as 'anachronistic: much too modern for the period' (White 2009). Rose agrees that Malouf has Priam speak in a way that is 'decidedly un-Homeric, too modern to convince' (*Australian Book Review*). Taking an opposite view, Mendelsohn (2010) praises the blend of past and present themes in *Ransom*. In his view, it enlarges the possibilities of Homer's *Iliad*: 'This is tampering at its very best', with Malouf exploring the 'wishful possibility that the two sides might not have to fight anymore, that we can break out of characters and create a new history.' Such a reading might be favoured by those who like literature to be relevant to contemporary issues, such as how to solve social and political conflicts.

The introduction of the carter Somax and his mules is regarded by some as the 'centrepiece of the entire novel' (White 2009) and by others as an 'eccentric (an unpersuasive) diversion' (Coates 2010). Some critics see Somax as an early version of Homer, with the final pages revealing Malouf's concern with how history turns into myth and stories into epics.

Ransom has been described as 'a rich meditation on literary genre – on the difference between Homer's form, the epic, with its encrustations of formulaic language, its strict codes of heroic behaviour, and its fated ending, and Malouf's own form, the novel' (Mendelsohn). Others regard it as a relatively short work, a 'novella' whose poetic structure suggests an extended prose poem. Some critics have found Part I rather slow in pace, with the plot only reviving when Priam starts on his journey. Others note that the transformation in Priam and Achilles' way of thinking differs significantly from Homer's focus on force in human history.

Two interpretations

'In *Ransom*, David Malouf shows how an ancient work of literature can be refreshed for a modern audience, but it is important to know Homer's *Iliad* to really appreciate Malouf's achievement.'

Ransom offers a view of war that shows how ingrained aggression is in human history. This tale could be set in a modern conflict, especially one in which neither side will give in to the other. The novel points to the danger of cities and civilisations being destroyed if we cannot find peaceful ways to end disputes. There are certainly advantages in being familiar with *The Iliad*, in knowing the characters and how the war ends. Legends about Troy are interesting in themselves and give depth to reading the novel.

The characterisation of Achilles and Priam can be compared in the two texts, highlighting the way Malouf shows the reader the psychology of the warrior-hero, Achilles, in greater depth than found in Homer. He is more like a modern individual who feels caught in a dilemma. The reader can sympathise with him even though his main focus is on fighting. We see that he is more than just a brutal bully. The way the novel describes his mother's influence on him is especially notable for its difference to Homer's language, as colourful as that is. From the opening passage of Part I the reader is aware that Malouf is using a very different genre from that of Homer.

Priam has experiences in *Ransom* that he does not have in *The Iliad*. His journey with Somax (a new character) and the mules (also new) is one of the highlights of the novel and shows Malouf's ability to enter and expand upon Homer's story. It would be hard to appreciate Malouf's additions to this episode if you were not familiar with *The Iliad*. He brings a lighter, comic-pastoral tone that balances the tragic scenes in the book. The ending of *Ransom* emphasises the mixed nature of storytelling where history, legend and fiction can all blend. While epics laid a wonderful foundation in western literature, the centuries since have opened up even more possibilities for stories to be shaped to show human life. Being able to appreciate Homer's *Iliad* as well as Malouf's *Ransom* gives readers a sense of the creative energy to be found in such imaginative stories. We can learn from them as well as enjoy them.

'Appreciating *Ransom* does not rely on knowledge of *The Iliad*. It creates its own world and speaks to readers on its own terms.'

Ransom is a novel that guides the reader to appreciate the flow of the plot and the characters as they are presented. The five parts are like a drama or a symphony that invites the reader to compare and contrast the themes, tone and style of each section. The novel blends tragedy and comedy and offers its own view of the world. If anything, it is best to read Malouf's earlier poetry and prose to understand *Ransom*, rather than *The Iliad*. It forms an important link with his body of work and connects with novels such as *An Imaginary Life*, *Fly Away Peter* and *Remembering Babylon*. The reader can sense that Malouf is a poet, so reading his poems such as 'Stooping to Drink' and 'Episode from an Early War' is also helpful.

It is useful to note the complex characterisations and underlying patterns of imagery, such as the way water, earth, air and fire are connected with different characters. Malouf's view of the intricate connection between our bodies and our minds is made clear in these terms. Achilles, for example, is described as being of earth and water, a blend of his parents' natures. It is not necessary to know *The Iliad* to understand this.

Whether *Ransom* is the same or different to *The Iliad* will not make much difference to the enjoyment of most readers. We expect a novel to be successful on its own terms and to offer a complete experience in itself without reference to earlier works. Like a good film or painting, a novel should provide a richly imagined experience that the reader can get inside. If Malouf had relied on readers knowing *The Iliad*, he might have written differently to avoid offending people with the changes he has made. He clearly has not worried about this possible criticism but has created a novel he finds satisfying in its own way. Readers should accept this too and value each work for itself.

QUESTIONS & ANSWERS

This section focuses on your own analytical writing on the text and gives you strategies for producing high quality responses in your coursework and exam essays.

Essay writing – an overview

An essay is a formal and serious piece of writing that presents your point of view on the text, usually in response to a given essay topic. Your 'point of view' in an essay is your interpretation of the meaning of the text's language, structure, characters, situations and events, supported by detailed analysis of textual evidence.

Analyse – don't summarise

In your essays it is important to avoid simply summarising what happens in a text:

- A **summary** is a description or paraphrase (retelling in different words) of the characters and events. For example: 'Macbeth has a horrifying vision of a dagger dripping with blood before he goes to murder King Duncan'.
- An **analysis** is an explanation of the real meaning or significance that lies 'beneath' the text's words (or images in a film). For example: 'Macbeth's vision of a bloody dagger shows how deeply uneasy he is about the violent act he is contemplating – as well as his sense that supernatural forces are impelling him to act'.

A limited amount of summary is sometimes necessary to let your reader know which part of the text you wish to discuss. However, always keep this to a minimum and follow it immediately with your analysis (explanation) of what this part of the text is really telling us.

Plan your essay

Carefully plan your essay so that you have a clear idea of what you are going to say. A plan will ensure that your ideas flow logically, that your argument remains consistent and that you stay on the topic. An essay plan should be a list of **brief dot points** – no more than half a page. It includes:

- your central argument or main contention – a concise statement (usually in a single sentence) of your overall response to the topic. See 'Analysing a sample topic' for guidelines on how to formulate a main contention.
- three or four dot points for each paragraph indicating the main idea and evidence/examples from the text. Note that in your essay you will need to *expand* on these points and *analyse* the evidence.

Structure your essay

An essay is a complete, self-contained piece of writing. It has a clear beginning (the introduction), middle (several body paragraphs) and end (the last paragraph or conclusion). It should also have a central argument that runs throughout, linking each paragraph to form a coherent whole.

See examples of introductions and conclusions in the 'Analysing a sample topic' and 'Sample answer' sections.

The introduction establishes your overall response to the topic. It includes your main contention and outlines the main evidence you will refer to in the course of the essay. Write your introduction *after* you have done a plan and *before* you write the rest of the essay.

The body paragraphs argue your case – they present evidence from the text and explain how this evidence supports your argument. Each body paragraph needs:

- a strong **topic sentence** (usually the first sentence) that states the main point being made in the paragraph
- **evidence** from the text, including some brief quotations
- **analysis** of the textual evidence explaining its significance and **explanation** of how it supports your argument

- **links back to the topic** in one or more statements, usually towards the end of the paragraph.

Connect the body paragraphs so that your discussion flows smoothly. Use some linking words and phrases like 'similarly' and 'on the other hand', but don't start every paragraph like this. Another strategy is to use a significant word from the last sentence of one paragraph in the first sentence of the next.

Use key terms from the topic – or synonyms for them – throughout, so the relevance of your discussion to the topic is always clear.

The conclusion ties everything together and finishes the essay. It includes strong statements that emphasise your central argument and provide a clear response to the topic.

Avoid simply restating the points made earlier in the essay – this will end on a very flat note and imply that you have run out of ideas and vocabulary. The conclusion is meant to be a logical extension of what you have written, not just a repetition or summary of it. Writing an effective conclusion can be a challenge. Try using these tips:

- Start by linking back to the final sentence of the second-last paragraph – this helps your writing to 'flow', rather than just leaping back to your main contention straight away.
- Use synonyms and expressions with equivalent meanings to vary your vocabulary. This allows you to reinforce your line of argument without being repetitive.
- When planning your essay, think of one or two broad statements or observations about the text's wider meaning. These should be related to the topic and your overall argument. Keep them for the conclusion, since they will give you something 'new' to say but still follow logically from your discussion. The introduction will be focused on the topic, but the conclusion can present a wider view of the text.

Essay topics

1 'It is his view of Hector that Achilles must wrestle with if he is to achieve any peace of mind.' Do you agree?

2 'The most enjoyable part of the novel occurs after Somax and his mules appear. There is not much action until then.' Is this a view you share? Discuss the role of Somax in the novel.

3 Evaluate the role of Hecuba in the novel. How does she influence Priam's values and actions?

4 'Priam's journey to Achilles' camp provides a ransom for himself as well as for Hector.' Explain how Priam is changed by his experiences and why this occurs.

5 '*Ransom* focuses on a masculine world of heroes and warfare. There is only a minor role for the feminine.' Do you agree? What is your understanding of Malouf's representation of the feminine in the novel?

6 How is narrative point of view used in the novel to give the reader a range of perspectives on the idea of the hero?

7 "This old fellow, like most storytellers, is a stealer of other men's tales, of other men's lives." How does *Ransom* represent the value of telling stories?

8 "I come also as a hero of the deed that till now was never attempted." Discuss the significance of the theme of 'chance' in *Ransom*.

9 'Malouf's use of language and imagery in *Ransom* shows the value of appreciating what is around us every day.' Discuss this view with close reference to two or three key images in the novel and indicate their importance in the structure of the narrative.

10 "We're children of nature, my lord. Of earth, as well as of the gods." Is Somax's view of humanity important in *Ransom*? Explain your view.

Vocabulary for writing on *Ransom*

Narrative point of view: the perspective from which the story is being told at any point. Examples include the third-person narrator (he/she said) and the first-person narrator (I said). Note the blending of perspectives in *Ransom* where a third-person account moves in and out of a character's thoughts. The reader is brought very close to the character while also maintaining an outside view.

Imagery: patterns of words that use resources of language (e.g. simile, metaphor, sounds, sensory description) to give added depth to a scene, a character's way of thinking and actions in the story. For example, images of fire and redness are used to convey concepts such as war or violent death and the feelings associated with them.

Apprehend (verb): without words, characters sense the world around them in particular ways. For example, Priam apprehends that Achilles is experiencing strong emotion and kneels before him out of 'instant fellow feeling' (p.187). Achilles apprehends that Hector has died honourably and so his corpse is 'no longer an affront' to him (p.190). When a character knows something without words and almost before realising he *does* know it, then apprehension is at work. The knowledge that comes quickly and just before words form is an important feature of characterisation in *Ransom* and in Malouf's work overall. It is what he values highly as the 'inner' world of a character, the intuitive view from 'inside' the character's mind that leads to growth in understanding and then to action.

Comprehend: to understand ideas and concepts. For example, Somax comprehends that he is to be called Idaeus, the king's herald, even though he is not sure he likes the idea (p.98). Up until the day of his journey, Priam comprehends the importance that his role as king has for his people and acts accordingly in a formal, consistent manner so he is trusted by them.

Story-time: the time represented as actually passing in the story. For example, the action of *Ransom* occurs over one day and night and the morning of the next day. The story-time covered is a relatively short period, although the narrative also includes flashbacks and flash-forwards.

Narrative time (or discourse time): the proportion of the book devoted to telling specific parts of the story. For example, in Part I there is much narrative time given to recounting what happened in the past using the techniques of flashback (going into the past) and summary (a short retelling of events).

Setting: where the story is located. For example, the setting of Part II is the river Scamander and the plain near Troy.

Analysing a sample topic

Topic 1: 'It is his view of Hector that Achilles must wrestle with if he is to achieve any peace of mind.' Do you agree?

This topic asks you to state whether or not you agree with the proposition. Rather than focusing on Achilles' grief at Patroclus' death (the more obvious cause), it points to the way Achilles is thinking about Hector as a source of his dilemma. Before making a decision on a line of argument, a brief review of your reading of Part I and Part IV and the short section on Achilles in Part V will be essential. These are the parts of the novel on which the essay should focus, as they feature Achilles. Remember that Achilles is disturbed about two dead warriors – Patroclus and Hector. What happens in the meeting with Priam that moves Achilles to a calmer frame of mind? Why does agreeing to the ransom release Achilles from his turmoil in Part IV? Answering these questions will give direction to your line of argument. Use relevant brief quotations that support your view in the body paragraphs of your essay.

Begin by noticing the key phrases 'must wrestle with' and 'peace of mind' in the topic sentence. What do you think Achilles is trying to work out in Part I? Why does he want to hear the voice of his mother, Thetis? What is the nature of his difficulty? Remember that Achilles regards Hector as his enemy and killed him in revenge for the slaughter of Patroclus. Shouldn't that have settled the debt? Think about why Achilles has been dragging Hector's body around in the dust for the last eleven days. How does he feel after he does this? Does he feel guilt over the death of Patroclus (who died in his armour)? Has the loss of his companion made him reconsider his belief in the hero's death as the ideal for which he lives? In Part IV he finally accepts that he is no longer at war with Hector. Why has this only happened at this point and not earlier in the story? Is the novel offering a comment on Achilles' 'peace of mind' when the action has a flash-forward to Neoptolemus killing Priam in an unheroic way?

Sample introduction *(assumes agreement with the proposition)*

Achilles has maintained his belief in the warrior-hero's role as his ideal for living and dying for nine long years of the Trojan War. After killing Hector in retaliation for the tragic death of Patroclus, he finds that ideal severely tested. Can he believe any longer in what he is doing? Is death really so heroic in war? Achilles focuses his grief and anger on the body of Hector. He drags it through the dust behind his chariot each day, breaking the customary code of honour for the dead. It is only when he releases Hector's body to Priam that his regains his peace of mind. It can be argued that rethinking his relationship with Hector is therefore essential for Achilles' peace and well-being. The opening scenes and Achilles' encounter that evening with Priam when he comes to ransom Hector provide the main evidence to support this view.

Body paragraph 1

Main point: Achilles' defilement of Hector's body shows he is wrestling with a dilemma. He is mourning deeply for Patroclus but even his elaborate burial ritual leaves Achilles numb and unsatisfied.

Relevant evidence for this point includes:

- the opening scene on the beach
- Achilles longs for his mother's softening influence
- Achilles' feelings after dragging Hector's body
- Achilles' understanding that Patroclus died while pretending to be him
- Achilles' unreasonable defilement of Hector's body.

Argument: Achilles' ongoing treatment of Hector shows the heart of his dilemma; revenge has not satisfied him. He needs something undefined that still escapes him.

Body paragraph 2

Main point: The unexpected meeting with Priam and his request to ransom Hector's body provide the situation needed to break Achilles' state of confusion.

Relevant evidence: In the Myrmidons' mess hut in Part IV:

- Achilles seems disengaged and listless
- a change comes over him as a lyre plays and he senses his mother's presence
- an unknown figure approaches
- the figure's identity is questioned
- Priam makes his request in an unexpected way
- Achilles responds positively.

Argument: The combination of his mother's presence and Priam's appeal to him as a father (as well as a son) makes Achilles change his mind; he realises that Hector was like himself – a hero bound to die.

Body paragraph 3

Main point: After agreeing to Priam's request, Achilles finds peace and comes to terms with his role as a warrior-hero.

Relevant evidence: As Achilles visits the body of Hector for the last time:

- his state of mind is calm
- he has gained a sense of Hector's accomplishment and his own to come
- he realises that he has finally found 'the true Achilles'.

Argument: Compassion and pity for Neoptolemus' situation and the memory of his own father's affection create a tender state of mind in which Achilles can share in the sorrows of his enemies. He broadens his view of being human. His anger at himself is released and he accepts the destiny chosen by him and for him. However, for his son who follows him to Troy, revenge results in shame rather than peace of mind.

Sample conclusion

The final view of Achilles shows him lifting his sword, the warrior's symbol, in all its power: it is 'metal from the depths of the earth made solid flame'. However, by shifting the focus of the narrative immediately to his son Neoptolemus' feeling of misery that 'will last forever', the heroic ideal is challenged. While Achilles has wrestled with his view of Hector and gained a victory over his confused feelings, his contentment is placed in the wider context of ongoing violence. The deeds of exceptional fighters like Hector and Achilles exact a high price on themselves and all around them, making 'peace of mind' hard to sustain.

SAMPLE ANSWER

Topic 5: '*Ransom* focuses on a masculine world of heroes and warfare. There is only a minor role for the feminine.' Do you agree? What is your understanding of Malouf's representation of the feminine in the novel?

In *Ransom* men such as Priam, Achilles, Hector and Agamemnon have supreme political and military power. They rule here as they did the epic world of Homer's *Iliad* on which the novel is based. Apart from Priam's wife (Hecuba), women seem to have relatively minor roles. There is 'women's work' for them to do, such as cooking pikelets for Somax (Part III) and washing Hector's corpse (Part IV), two very domestic chores. However, this is only one way of understanding ideas of masculinity and femininity in the novel. By adding further depth to the two main characters, Priam and Achilles, Malouf weaves into his storytelling images of 'masculine' and 'feminine' that complement each other. These images feature energy in motion and are often taken from nature (flowing water, moving air). They are a reminder that goddesses portrayed as female (Thetis and Iris) have key roles in the action. In the myths and legends that hover in the background of Malouf's novel, 'feminine' characters often transcend roles traditionally assigned by biological gender.

In the personality of Achilles both masculine and feminine facets are made clear at the start of Part I and are linked to nature. 'Earth is his element', but so is the fluid world of his mother, the sea goddess Thetis. He is constantly drawn to the ever-changing energy of oceans, pools and streams and can sense his mother's element in his body and mind. This energy-flow balances what has become hard and manly in him as he has trained to be a great warrior. Locked in his grief after Patroclus is killed by Hector, Achilles waits at dawn to hear his mother's voice. When he is challenged by Priam that same night to ransom Hector's body, Achilles senses his mother's presence. The climax in Part IV requires him to overcome his heart-felt despair. With lyre music playing (suggesting the god Hermes' favour) Achilles feels the particles within him 'tumble and swarm'. He becomes open to Priam's plea and 'something in him has freed and fallen way'. It is what the novel represents as feminine energy that allows Achilles to be restored. He feels 'a perfect order of body, heart, occasion'.

Priam has closer formal contact with women from day to day than Achilles in his makeshift war camp, where their only role is to cater for the basic needs of men. Priam speaks in a close, loving way with Hecuba (Part II) and values her respect. In fact, he can be scared of her ('He has always been afraid of this controlled rage in her'). Priam has had many wives and children, although his role as king has tended to make him formal and distant from expressing true emotion before other people. His world is full of ceremony and artifice. While Hecuba and, to a lesser extent, his prophetess daughter Cassandra have power in the court, Priam separates himself from talk about birth and children ('This kind of women's talk unnerves him').

During his journey with Somax to Achilles' camp, Priam apprehends the feminine in a fresh way. He becomes interested in the simple details of a woman's everyday life (Somax tells of his daughter-in-law and little grand-daughter). He enjoys a tasty pikelet and imagines them being cooked. He becomes curious about things he might have previously ignored. He enjoys Somax's chatter as a form of storytelling he has not known before. He apprehends the 'prattling world' of nature in a more attentive way and likes the black mule Beauty. He dips his feet in the river and watches 'water as it went hopping over the stones and turned back on itself and hopped again'.

Priam's new experiences connect images of Thetis' softening, fluid influence on Achilles with Priam's closer attention to all that is going on around him. It helps him to speak in a genuine, moving way when he meets Achilles. He comes as a human being, a father. Achilles, his compassionate, fluid side at work, accepts Priam's ransom. Both men are open to each other because they have felt what the novel represents as 'feminine' at work within them, changing them.

Images of masculine and feminine complement each other in the ending of *Ransom*. Both Priam and Somax look forward to a homecoming that will bring them together with the women they love. Priam thinks with affection of the young woman who made the pikelets and is delighted to see Hecuba waiting for him on the walls of Troy. Even though she opposed him, he has undertaken this daring quest for her too. To take a chance, as he has done, is to trust that things can be otherwise. Like water flowing over pebbles (a recurring image), events can tumble around and reform. In *Ransom*, the reader can look beneath traditional male and female social roles, bequeathed by Homer's epic tradition, and notice that images of masculine and feminine balance each other in nature to create a fuller view of human beings.

REFERENCES & READING

Text

Malouf, David, *Ransom*, North Sydney: Knopf/Random House Australia, 2009.

Related essays by David Malouf

'Men and Gods Behaving Badly', *The Australian Literary Review,* 4 March 2009.

'Relative Freedom: *The Tempest*', Sydney: English Association Sydney, 1973.

'A Mirror for our Times', *ANU Reporter*, Summer 2009, 13.

Interviews with David Malouf

'UNSWriting presents David Malouf', 20 April 2010, UNSWTV: University Services. https://tv.unsw.edu.au/video/unswriting-presents-david-malouf

ABC Radio National, 'The Book Show', 'David Malouf's *Ransom*', 1 April 2009. http://www.abc.net.au/radionational/programs/bookshow/david-maloufs-ransom/3052444

'David Malouf in the House of Writing, 1–6', The Red Room Company, The Wordshed, 2006. http://redroomcompany.org/projects/wordshed

DVD on Malouf's life and works to 1996

David Malouf: An Imaginary Life: the inner world of an extraordinary writer. dir. Don Featherstone, Film Australia, 1996.

CD recording of Malouf reading his poetry

David Malouf Reads from Poems 1959–89, Glebe, NSW: Tall Poppies, 1996.

Selected reviews of *Ransom*

Coates, Steve, 'Troy Story', *Sunday Book Review, New York Times*, January 22 2010.

Holland, Tom, '*Ransom* by David Malouf', *Guardian*, December 19 2009.

Manguel, Alberto, 'Review of *Ransom*', *Australian Literary Review*, April 1 2009.

Mendelsohn, Daniel, 'Epic Endeavours', *New Yorker*, April 5 2010.

Rose, Peter, 'The Very Edge of Things', *Australian Book Review*, May 2009.

Smith, Yvonne, 'Beauty's Clear, Round Eye', *Southerly* 69:1 2009, Long Paddock.

White, Edmund, 'Classic Case of Nobility Meeting Reality', *Books of the Times, New York Times*, December 29 2009.

On Malouf's work

Indyk, Ivor, *David Malouf*, Melbourne: Oxford University Press, 1993.

Neilsen, Philip, *Imagined Lives: A Study of David Malouf*, St Lucia: University of Queensland Press, 1996.

Nettelbeck, Amanda, *Reading David Malouf*, Melbourne: Oxford University Press, 1995.

Randall, Don, *David Malouf*, Manchester and New York: Manchester University Press, 2007.

Classical background

Homer, *The Iliad*, trans. E.V. Rieu, revised edition, London: Penguin Classics, 2003.

Alexander, Caroline, *The War That Killed Achilles: The True Story of Homer's* Iliad *and the Trojan War,* London: Viking, 2009.

Troy and its history

Troy Homepage, University of Cincinnati. http://cerhas.uc.edu/troy/

Film/DVD

Troy, dir. Wolfgang Petersen, Warner Bros Picture, 2004, starring Brad Pitt.